SAINT-GERMAIN-DES-PRÉS

ALSO BY JOHN BAXTER

Five Nights in Paris
Paris at the End of the World
The Perfect Meal
The Most Beautiful Walk in the World
Von Sternberg
Carnal Knowledge
Immoveable Feast
We'll Always Have Paris
A Pound of Paper
Science Fiction in the Cinema
Buñuel
Fellini
Stanley Kubrick
Steven Spielberg
Woody Allen
George Lucas
De Niro

TRANSLATED BY JOHN BAXTER

My Lady Opium by Claude Farrère
Morphine by Jean-Louis Dubut de Laforest
The Diary of a Chambermaid by Octave Mirbeau
Gamiani, or Two Nights of Excess by Alfred de Musset

SAINT-GERMAIN-DES-PRÉS

Paris's Rebel Quarter

John Baxter

HARPER PERENNIAL

NEW YORK • LONDON • TORONTO • SYDNEY • NEW DELHI • AUCKLAND

HARPER PERENNIAL

HarperCollins books may be purchased for educational, business, or sales promotional use. For information, please email the Special Markets Department at SPsales@harpercollins.com.

FIRST EDITION

Designed by Jamie Kerner

Map by Tony Foster

Library of Congress Cataloging-in-Publication Data has been applied for.

ISBN 978-0-06-243190-5

16 17 18 19 20   RRD   10 9 8 7 6 5 4 3 2 1

*Pour Marie-Dominique and Louise
et la vie en rose.*

Cities are bibles of stone. This city possesses no single dome, roof or pavement which does not convey some message of alliance or of union, and which does not offer some lesson, example or advice. Let the people of all the world come to this prodigious alphabet of monuments, of tombs and of trophies to learn peace and unlearn the meaning of hatred. Let them be confident. For Paris has proven itself. To have once been Lutece and to have become Paris— what could be a more magnificent symbol? To have been mud and to have become spirit!

VICTOR HUGO

Contents

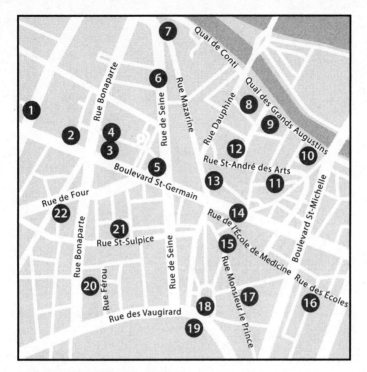

Saint-Germain-Des-Prés

SAINT-GERMAIN-DES-PRÉS

INTRODUCTION

A VILLAGE IN A CITY

Where a man feels at home, outside of where he's born,
is where he's meant to go.
ERNEST HEMINGWAY, *GREEN HILLS OF*
AFRICA

I GREW UP IN CITIES. I NEVER EXPECTED TO SETTLE DOWN in a village.

That said, this village isn't like many others.

"Villages" today are often marketing gimmicks: a few shops done up in antique style, and actors in costume urging you to step in and buy something you don't want.

Our village of Saint-Germain is real. It began as all true villages do, when men and women closed ranks against the unknown. After agreeing on the limits of their community, they built some kind of wall, appointed a few neighbors to represent them, others to stand guard.

Natural borders define the true village—usually a river on one side, the highway passing by on the other, with, to the east, the fields they cultivate by day and, to the west, the church to which they look for solace, for learning, for help in sickness and war.

Saint-Germain has all of those. Even today, when it's embedded in a city, we cling to that pride, that sense of belonging—and, admittedly, to the old suspicions. Standing on our frontier, we look across the street at our neighbors and think, "Oh, *them*."

It can't be a coincidence that a man from Saint-Germain, Guy Debord, first proposed the theory of psychogeography: a sense of place so fundamental that it infuses emotion as powerfully as a drug.

Scots swear that, as their car crosses the border with England, they experience a bump. Actor Robert De Niro, born in New York's Greenwich Village, "just doesn't feel comfortable" above Fourteenth Street. The residents of some South London districts are so recognizable by style and accent that they have a uniform: velvet suits covered in pearl buttons, Pearly Kings and Queens.

And don't try telling a Virginian that the Mason-Dixon Line is just a "geographical convention" or you may have an argument on your hands.

Our village has no walls—not physical ones anyway—
nor is the accent particularly distinctive. Nobody wears a
uniform. Unless you count political demonstrations, we
do not parade. There are no souvenir shops selling scented
candles or snow domes; look in vain for "I [heart] Saint-
Germain" T-shirts. We do not advertise. We just tell visitors "Look for yourselves," and for those who do, our
secrets reveal themselves.

They soon notice, for instance, that, even though it's
barely half the size of New York's Central Park and no
bigger than Hyde Park in London, Saint-Germain has sheltered some of civilization's greatest personalities.

Ours is the village of those archetypal great lovers
Héloïse and Abelard; of Pablo Picasso and Arthur Rimbaud; of F. Scott Fitzgerald and Ernest Hemingway; of
Inspector Maigret and Napoleon Bonaparte; the *Rights of
Man* and *The Sun Also Rises* and "La Vie en Rose" and *La
Bohème*; of Gertrude Stein, Simone de Beauvoir, and Jean-
Paul Sartre; Juliette Gréco, café society, the new wave of
cinema; of existentialism—and, forgetting for a moment
mind and soul, long afternoons in crumpled sheets, lunches
that last till sunset, baguettes with cheese, a *café crème* or a
glass of Bordeaux shared with someone close on a *bateau
mouche* as it glides under Pont Neuf, pivots in the eddy at

the foot of the Île Saint-Louis, and heads back downstream under the disapproving eye of Notre Dame.

Our streets have seen history made and unmade. In 1789, they ran with blood as our village joined with others to put down a corrupt society. In May 1968, the youth of Paris poured out of the universities and, meeting in our local theatre, remade Europe in a few weeks, really just for the hell of it. It was, remarked a surprised historian, the only known revolution in which nobody died.

But revolution here comes in all sizes. Just down our street, in a little bookshop, a small but determined woman from Princeton, New Jersey, took upon herself the burden of publishing James Joyce's *Ulysses*, the novel that transfigured literature.

You might think that every original thought would long since have been wrung from these stones, these lanes and courtyards, and that one's mind would run off over the sea of metal roofs of Paris into wider fields and skies.

But one does not *tire* here. There is always more to experience because each day more is made.

Nothing in our village ever dies. It is a living museum of what we can create, both at our finest moments and our worst.

We call our village Saint-Germain—not pronounced *Jermayne*, by the way, but like "Jerman" and emphasizing the second syllable: *Jer-MAN*. We're a little touchy about that. Otherwise, with occasional exceptions, we're hospitable and welcome visitors.

You should come. You might even stay a while. I did.

The first half-hour in Paris is sometimes more painful than pleasant. Even veteran travelers suffer from the feeling that everyone is shouting at them because they are slow and stupid. They are torn between the fear of seeming ignorant, or being humiliated should they dispense the wrong-sized tip. But once the headlong plunge is taken, there comes the first mounting excitement.

KAYE WEBB, RONALD SEARLE'S *PARIS SKETCHBOOK*

I first came to Paris in 1969. Signs of the previous May's troubles were everywhere—the stumps of felled trees along the boulevards; streets where cobbles had been torn up to fling at the police and militia—but the disturbances were already being minimized, downgraded from a revolution to mere *événements* (events).

Ernest Hemingway, Henry Miller, James Joyce, and the rest of the Lost Generation had long since moved on, but the Beat Generation had taken their place, with Jack Kerouac, William Burroughs, and Allen Ginsberg living and socializing in, if not the same hotels and cafés they had patronized, then places very like them.

For anyone ambitious to be an artist or writer, Paris remained the place one came to discover oneself. Most came the cheapest way. In 1969, that generally meant a ship—tramp steamers, refurbished prewar liners on their last crossings before the scrap yard, even repatriated wartime Liberty ships perilously ferrying munitions back from Europe.

The more fortunate, traveling from New York, made the trip in a week. For me, the voyage from Australia meant not five days at sea but thirty.

Before World War II, our ship, the *Australis*, had been the SS *America*. Its new owners, a Greek company, not only changed the name but subdivided its cabins to take three times the original complement of one thousand passengers, even if some had to bunk with the crankshaft.

Four or five times a year, this floating tenement sailed from Southampton to Sydney, packed with Europeans fleeing fogs and rain and seeking a new life in the sun. On the return trip, it carried Australians bored with unremitting sunshine and eager for old-world sophistication. In December 1969, that group included my girlfriend and myself.

A few weeks after landing in Britain, we made our first excursion across the English Channel. It wasn't easy. With Britain still dithering about joining a federated Europe—

it's dithering still—we had to acquire a French visa, exchange pounds for francs, travel by train to Dover, let customs officials paw through our luggage, make the rough ferry crossing to Calais, then take another train for Paris.

By the time we hauled our bags up the steps from the Saint-Michel underground station, it was late afternoon. Office workers jammed the pavements, fixated on getting home. Buses, cars, and motorbikes poured down boulevard Saint-Michel to tussle with more vehicles streaming along the quays of the Seine. If the traffic halted even momentarily, hundreds of pedestrians plunged into it, indifferent to the ding-ding-ding of the buses' warning bells.

Our first glimpse of a Parisian monument was the cathedral of Notre Dame, just across the Seine. After the serenity of London's Saint Paul's, its Gothic arches radiated an alien arrogance.

Rearing above the chaos on the far side of Place Saint-Michel, a giant sword-wielding archangel Michael crushed Lucifer beneath his feet while two dragons spouted water from gaping jaws. How unlike Australian fountains, whose lithe nymphs and muscular huntsmen looked like surfers who'd briefly left the sand in search of an ice cream.

Why this belligerence? I wondered. What made the French so angry?

Taking refuge in the first side street, we found ourselves in another century. The cobbles on which we stumbled were laid when Victor Hugo, if not François Villon, walked here. Though cafés and restaurants clamored for attention on every side, the buildings above their gaudy facades leaned and sagged, supported, it seemed, by nothing but centuries of grime.

The few street signs were either too small and high up to be readable, or blocked by café awnings. Appeals in our broken French for directions met with indifferent stares. Apparently the cheerful English-speaking Parisians of the movies didn't exist outside Hollywood's central casting.

Instead, housewives with bulging string bags jostled us, and disheveled young men shouldered past. The only person to acknowledge our existence was a shuffling tramp who spoke the international language of the doleful expression and the extended palm.

It took us a while to realize that some of the buildings around us housed hotels. None displayed porticos or doormen, just dark entrances squeezed between shops and cafés and with inconspicuous brass plates with lettering blurred by generations of polishing.

Choosing the Hôtel Splendide Saint-Germain at random, we edged our luggage down a narrow unlit corridor into a tiny reception area, its only furniture a lone dusty armchair, clearly unused since the reign of Louis XVI.

The desk clerk didn't hide his impatience with our fumbling French. We came to know his heavy-lidded stare, directed just above our heads. French waiters, shop assistants, and bureaucrats had been perfecting it for centuries. As far back as 1830, the novelist Stendhal advised those serving the public that "a melancholy air can never be the right thing. What you want is a *bored* air. If you are melancholy, it must be because *you* want something; there is something in which you have not succeeded. It is showing your inferiority. If you are bored, on the other hand, it is the person who has tried in vain to please you who is inferior."

Left in no doubt of our inferiority, we exchanged our passports for a room key attached to a wooden slab that made it too bulky to steal. A tiny elevator shuddered up three floors, delivering us to a room with seven corners, none of them right angles. A sagging double bed, a bureau, and a wardrobe comprised the only furniture. A diagram glued to the door showed the location of the communal bathroom and toilet, and, in closely typed and impenetrable French, explained the rules regarding the use of hot water.

Not exactly four-star accommodation. And yet . . . what did it matter? We were in Paris!

Leaning out the window, we stared down in delight on three cafés, every table packed with arguing, laughing, gesticulating Parisians. Waiters wove among them, delivering coffees and glasses of *vin rouge*. Of the conversation, we understood nothing except that what mattered here, above everything else, was talk. To raise one's voice, to wave one's hands, to argue and improvise—clearly there was, for these people, no greater pleasure.

Well, perhaps one . . .

Paris, the capital of talk, was also the capital of sex, and the bed, though lumpy, had been made so by generations of lovers. Could there be a more potent aphrodisiac? We raced to see who could undress more quickly. The babble from two floors below, not to mention the smoke from un-filtered Gauloises, floated through a window over which we didn't bother to pull the curtains, even though we might be visible from the hotel opposite. Far from shy, we even relished the sense of an audience. It was, after all, Paris—and, better still, its least inhibited quarter. The magic of Saint-Germain had begun to work.

Can that really have been twenty-five years ago? Since then, I've married—not the girlfriend with whom I made that first visit but a Frenchwoman, Marie-Dominique, and a Parisienne at that, from Saint-Germain. Together, we raised a child, Louise. To my surprise, I found myself the newest member of an extended French family who could trace its roots to the emperor Charlemagne. For the first time in my life, I was Home.

✳ · 1 · ✳

STICKS AND STONES

We shape our buildings; thereafter they shape us.
WINSTON CHURCHILL

CONSIDERING ITS CULTURAL AND HISTORICAL IMPORTANCE, one expects Saint-Germain, a crooked oblong at the northern end of the sixth of Paris's twenty municipalities or *arrondissements*, to be larger. Yet it measures only two square kilometers—three-quarters of a square mile.

Officially it's bounded to the east by boulevard Saint-Michel, to the west by rue des Saints-Pères, to the north by the Seine, and to the south by rue de Vaugirard. But any attempt to define its limits can ignite a mutiny. What about the Sorbonne, for example? Should Paris's oldest university have been excluded because it's on the "wrong" side of boulevard Saint-Michel? And what of the Latin Quarter? A maze of narrow lanes once occupied by Latin-speaking religious schools, it also lies east of boulevard Saint-Michel.

Its supporters insisted, however, that, in spirit at least, it deserved to belong.

Others argued for the inclusion of the northern fringe of the Jardin du Luxembourg, just across rue de Vaugirard. Generations of lovers had slipped inside the high metal palings to lose themselves in its shrubbery. They continue to do so today, indifferent to the sweating joggers who puff by only a meter away on the track running between the railings and the bushes. Surely, argued opponents of limitation, this zone, drenched in so much ancient passion, deserved at least provisional status as a part of the *quartier*.

Why compete to live in a shabby, overpopulated corner of the city? Because, argued its residents, Saint-Germain preserved Paris as it used to be, having escaped the modernization ordered by Emperor Napoleon III and carried out by Georges-Eugène "Baron" Haussmann between 1853 and 1870.

No corner of Saint-Germain typifies the district more than an obscure alley called the Cour du Commerce Saint-André. Barely visible from boulevard Saint-Germain and dating from 1776, this cobbled lane of leaning buildings and ancient facades, terminating in a covered arcade, has barely changed in four centuries. If any thoroughfare illustrates the heritage of our village, this is it.

Why did Haussmann's demolition crews leave such

places intact? The reasons were both social and architectural. Though the neighborhood's older buildings dated from the 1600s, most remained structurally sound, thanks to a construction method that used beams from the city's most common tree, the chestnut, which is almost impervious to damp, fire, or termites.

To make a wall, builders created a framework of the wooden beams called *poutres*, plugged the gaps with rubble, then finished it with plaster reinforced with horsehair. Virtually immune to subsidence, such buildings flexed and sagged but seldom collapsed. If you demolished even one, however, those on either side tended to slump into the gap. To modernize Saint-Germain, Haussmann would have had to level whole blocks. Since the emperor required his wide thoroughfares mainly as a means of deploying artillery and infantry in the event of a revolution, he compromised. One new avenue, the east-west boulevard Saint-Germain, was driven through the district, and another, the north-south boulevard Saint-Michel, along one edge. Otherwise he left the *quartier* and its belligerent natives undisturbed.

Paris sprawls across a river valley that the Seine, socially and culturally, divides as decisively as the Hudson severs

Manhattan from New Jersey and the Danube separates Buda from Pest.

The Right Bank owns the valley floor, ensuring it has the most spacious apartments, the widest avenues and most generous sidewalks. It boasts the Élysée Palace—France's White House—and its premier theatrical venues, the Comédie-Française and Palais Garnier. The most luxurious hotels, the most select shopping streets—Champs-Élysées, rue de la Paix, Place Vendôme, and avenue Matignon—are all Rive Droite.

Cross the Seine, however, and the streets become narrow. Houses lean to cut off the sun. As sidewalks contract, roadways are transformed into pedestrian promenades where open-air markets sell fruit, vegetables, bread, ham, sausage, and, of course, cheese. You are in Saint-Germain.

For centuries, literary and political figures have gathered here to argue, expound, and write. Leaders of political and philosophical thought made it their home. Revolutions were hatched here, not only on issues of social change but on fashion, publishing, jazz, cuisine.

It took no intellect to choose Saint-Germain as the place to live. Since the eighteenth century, rebels, misfits, dissidents, pornographers, and troublemakers had congregated here. Close to the city walls, it was remote from the eyes of authority.

Locals believed the presence of these radical elements made their corner of the city busier, more colorful, more vital. Citizens of the Rive Droite saw it differently. They never forgot that the revolution of 1789 incubated in Saint-Germain. Danton, Robespierre, Marat, Desmoulins, and its other leaders plotted in the Café Procope, the back door of which faced the printery where Jean-Paul Marat published his virulently antimonarchist journal, *L'Ami du Peuple*. A few houses away, Dr. Joseph-Ignace Guillotin perfected the killing machine that would bear his name.

For intellectuals and artists, to endure the deficiencies of Saint-Germain became a point of pride. Living like a common laborer conferred a sort of nobility. In 1920, the sixth *arrondissement*, of which Saint-Germain is a part, housed about a hundred thousand people—twice as many as today.

But its inhabitants got only what they paid for. Only half the homes had electricity, or water on tap. Jugs and buckets were filled from wells in the courtyard and lugged upstairs. Private toilets were a luxury. In rooming houses, two or three filthy lavatories served fifty. Most people kept a chamber pot under the bed and emptied it each morning—sometimes out the window, with a casual *"Gardez l'eau"* ("Watch the water") to anyone who might be walking below.

Fetching water from the common pump, St. Germain, 1920s.

With water so scarce, bathing became a luxury. Napoleon Bonaparte often rose at two a.m. and, to the despair of his servants, demanded a hot bath, an affectation that astonished his subjects. A particularly fastidious Parisian might visit a public bathhouse weekly, or summon one of the itinerant bath-men who cruised the streets. Hauling a collapsible canvas or metal tub to your apartment, they filled it with water heated on your kitchen stove and left the family to enjoy a good wallow.

Most people, however, followed the lead of England's Queen Elizabeth I, who, as one courtier revealed, "bathed twice a year—even when she didn't need to." Paradoxically, Napoleon, despite his insistence on personal hygiene, relished the natural scents of a woman. Days before returning from battle, he wrote ahead to his new wife Joséphine, "Don't wash. I'm coming."

Inevitably, vermin flourished in the slums of Saint-Germain. In any European city, one was never farther than

Itinerant bath man.

a meter from a rat. Before bed, women routinely shook out their underwear over a dish of water. Fleas tumbled out like grains of pepper. Head lice were so common that mothers shaved their sons bald during summer.

Roaches and bedbugs, though impossible to exterminate, could at least be kept at bay. As British writer George Orwell explained in his gloomily informative *Down and Out in Paris and London*, he set fire to a dish of sulfur, sealed his doors and windows, and left for the day. The fumes drove the bugs into his neighbors' rooms—but only until they bought their own sulfur and sent them back.

Tuberculosis was rife, and incurable. Likewise syphilis and other sexually transmitted diseases. Prostitutes and pickpockets cruised public dance halls, the *bals musettes*. *Apache* gangsters mugged pedestrians at knifepoint and fought bloody turf wars in the streets. Opium, hashish, and cocaine, known as *chnouf*, were freely available, as was bootleg absinthe, which could make you blind or drive you mad.

Danger and squalor, however, helped create the ferment that produced great art. Artists or writers living in rented rooms spent as little time there as possible. Instead, they headed to the café. In its *toilette*, they washed, even shaved, took a *café crème* and a croissant at the *zinc*, or bar, and read the paper—then, as now, offered free to regular clients. Taking a table, they worked all morning, left for lunch, but returned for a *digestif*, after which the café became their office, a place to meet people of the same profession or inclination.

All that changed as the *sans-culottes* found not only their trousers but also the shoes, coats, and ties to go with them. During the boom of the late nineteenth century, the former poor metamorphosed into the new bourgeoisie. Saint-Germain became Paris's SoHo, Bloomsbury, Westwood. Rooming houses were reborn as hotels and apartment buildings. Butchers' and bakers' shops became boutiques. *Poutres*, once a sign of rustic construction, to be hidden under plaster, emerged as a valued indication of antiquity. Paris's cheapest place to live was now the most expensive. Today, a single square meter in Saint-Germain costs a minimum of US$20,000, and an apartment of even modest size will set you back $1 million.

LE COUR DU COMMERCE SAINT-ANDRÉ

Le Cour du Commerce Saint-André (arcade end).

From the huge "Belgian block" cobbles, later re-placed by Haussmann with smaller machine-cut granite cubes, to its leaning buildings built of plaster and chestnut, this lane preserves a fragment of eighteenth-century Saint-Germain. The workshops that once occupied it are now restaurants, but enough sites remain to evoke the 1789 revolution that transformed France.

- At no. 6, harpsichord maker Tobias Schmidt and Dr. Joseph-Ignace Guillotin perfected the guillotine, on which hundreds of thousands would die until France abandoned capital punishment in 1981. Ironically, Guillotin opposed the death penalty, and hoped his machine, by mechanizing executions, would bore the mob into supporting abolition. In fact, the possibility of decapitation on production line principles ignited the mass killings of the revolution known as the Terror that left as many as forty thousand dead.
- At no. 8, a round stone tower, part of the old city walls, housed the printery of publisher Jean-Paul Marat.
- Just beyond no. 8, a short lane leads to the gated community of the Cour de Rohan, formerly the Paris residence of the bishop of Rouen. Just above and to the left of the gate is the one-time studio of painter Balthasar Kłossowski, a.k.a. Balthus. The apartment was also used in the Leslie Caron film *Gigi*, as the home of Gigi's grandmother.

In the arcade at the bottom of the *passage* under the glass roof, a café on the left displays a rare visible example of classic eighteenth-century construction, with chestnut beams and plaster.

2

THE BODY IN THE BATH

Nothing in his life became him like the leaving of it.
WILLIAM SHAKESPEARE, *MACBETH*

JOURNALIST AND POLITICIAN JEAN-PAUL MARAT WAS among the more gifted of those who led the French Revolution, though also the most fanatical. Described as "a horribly ugly little man, almost a dwarf," he seemed "consumed with hatred and envy," exacerbated by a chronic skin disease, the irritation of which could only be relieved by soaking in a bath of water mixed with either oatmeal or vinegar.

Long before 1789, Marat had traveled widely, building an international reputation as a physician and scientist. Following the revolution, he was elected to the National Convention, joining the faction known as the Montagnards, or Mountain. From his printery in the Cour du Commerce Saint-André, he launched a newspaper, *L'Ami du Peuple* (*The Friend of the People*). Radical even by revolutionary standards, it urged mass executions of anyone associated with the aristocracy and the church.

On July 13, 1793, twenty-five-year-old Marie-Anne Charlotte de Corday d'Armont called at his home on rue des Écoles, a few minutes' walk from his printery. Although a member of the Girondin faction, Marat's most aggressive opponents, she promised details of a plot being hatched against the Montagnards in the northern city of Caen.

Revolutionary etiquette dictated that, since all citizens were equal, even public figures should be accessible to all. The note Corday handed to Marat's servant reminded him of this fact. It read *"Il suffit que je sois bien malheureuse pour avoir droit a votre bienveillance"*—"My unhappiness gives me the right to ask for your help."

Marat asked her to return that evening. When she did, his servants admitted her, even though he was in his bath. As he noted the names of the supposed anti-Montagnards in Caen, Marat assured her with sinister glee, "In eight hours, they will be on the guillotine!"

At this, she took a kitchen knife from under her skirts and plunged it into his heart. He died instantly.

Making no attempt to escape, she was seized and held for trial. But if she had expected Marat's death would end the persecution of the Girondins, she was mistaken. The next day, René-François Lebois, who took over as editor of *L'Ami du Peuple*, made an impassioned speech urging the death of all who opposed the Montagnards. "A conspiracy to assassinate our best, our firmest supporters, our faithful representatives has revealed itself," he said. "Already, yesterday a sacrilegious hand dared stab the firmest supporter, the most zealous defender of the people. It's time for the permanent guillotine." The speech helped bring about the mass slaughter known as the Terror, during which tens of thousands died, including the royal family.

Charlotte Corday preceded them on July 17, 1793, four days after the murder. It was customary for the assistant executioner to display the severed head of the victim to the crowd—evidence that justice had been done. In her case, however, the head was snatched by a carpenter named Legros who was repairing the guillotine.

Some still believed consciousness could survive in the brain even after decapitation. To test this hypothesis, Legros slapped Corday's cheeks as he held up the head. Watchers were shocked. Many claimed she blushed. Others reported an expression of "unequivocal indignation" on her face. Once Corday was found to have been a virgin, Legros was jailed for three months for taking liberties; murderess or not, she deserved to be treated with respect.

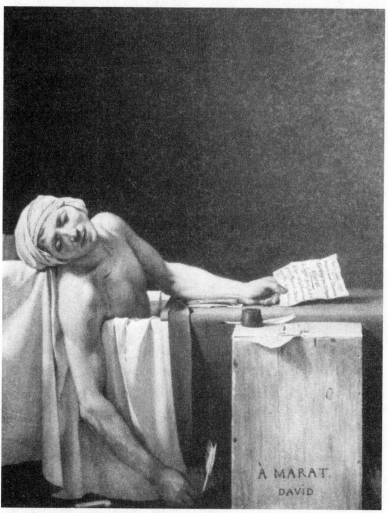

Marat Assassiné *by Jacques-Louis David*.

MARAT ASSASSINÉ (THE MURDER OF MARAT)

We remember Marat today almost entirely because of *Marat Assassiné*, the painting by Jacques-Louis David. A fellow Montagnard, David visited Marat the day before his death. With details of the house still sharp in his mind, he immediately began work, assuring the National Convention that he would show Marat favorably, as someone who died *"écrivant pour le bonheur du peuple"*—writing for the good of the people.

Marat Assassiné became one of the revolution's most famous images. A skilled propagandist, David included both authentic and invented details. The bath, the green carpet, and Marat's papers are all as he recalled them, but the fatal knife lies on the floor by the bath and not where Corday left it, buried in his chest. Nor does Marat exhibit signs of his unsightly disease. He is also shown clutching Corday's letter, whereas in reality he died with a copy of *L'Ami du Peuple* in his hand.

David borrowed from classicism to confer nobility on his subject. Marat's pose, particularly his dangling right arm, still holding a quill pen, recalled Renaissance pietàs showing the dead Christ in the arms of his mother, while a clear overhead light illuminates the entire image, giving the murder a sense of martyrdom.

The painting remained popular and much reproduced until the mass executions of the Terror culminated in Robespierre's death. Power in the exhausted nation passed to a committee of moderates known as the Directoire, or Directorate, which ruled until the rise of Napoleon.

Accused of complicity in the Terror, David fled to Belgium, and his more propagandist canvases disappeared—even more so when he returned to favor as Napoleon's preferred artist. Following David's death in 1825, his family tried without success to sell *Marat Assassiné*, finally making a gift of it to Belgium, which gave the artist refuge. It still hangs in the Royal Museum of Fine Arts in Brussels.

3

A TALE OF TWO CAFÉS

*My dear, at first I was uncertain whether the Dôme was
a place or a state of mind or a disease. It is all three.*
HENRY GORMAN, *"AT THE DÔME,"* 1929

To UNDERSTAND SAINT-GERMAIN, YOU NEED TO SEE THE
district as its neighbors did.

If residents of the Right Bank despised Saint-Germain,
they disliked Montparnasse even more. This was something on which people on both sides of the river could
agree: the hilltop village occupying the other half of the
sixth *arrondissement* was an embarrassment.

Montparnasse evolved over a century from a colony of
Italian masons who camped above the underground quar-
ries that supplied the stone that rebuilt Paris in the 1850s.
Returning with drays of debris from demolished slums,
they dumped it along the ridge, creating a giant rubbish
heap. Adding to the desolate atmosphere, the city's anon-

ymous dead rotted in mass graves in the nearby paupers' cemetery.

Students from the Quartier Latin who toiled up the hill in search of cheap home-brewed wine, then roistered around the village, drunkenly declaiming poetry to the city below, mockingly gave it the name of the mountain in ancient Greece on which the muses made their home: Parnassus.

Montparnasse never escaped its gaudy reputation. While Saint-Germain could boast a few wide squares and avenues, the Sorbonne and the church of Saint-Sulpice, the best Montparnasse could offer was a railroad depot and a boulevard lined with cafés and bars. Even when the paupers' graveyard became the Cimetière du Montparnasse, one of the best laid out in the city, a stigma lingered. True to type, the street running beside the cemetery wall, boulevard Edgar Quinet, sprouted rowdy cabarets, the lesbian club Le Monocle, and an upmarket brothel, Le Sphinx.

For expatriates, the outlaw reputation of Montparnasse proved its most potent attraction. Following World War I, its cafés became a magnet for tourists. So many foreigners settled there that they called the sixth *arrondissement* "the Quarter"—a zone, like the Casbah of Algiers, within which the rules of the surrounding city didn't apply.

Nobody who lived there needed to speak French.

Café du Dôme, 1920s.

Shopkeepers, waiters, barmen, and whores soon became fluent in English, although, just to be on the safe side, some cafés offered English menus, often comically mistranslated. When Le Sphinx opened in 1931, it produced a brochure explaining its services. American author Henry Miller, a regular client, wrote the English text. Offered payment in either cash or credit, he chose the latter and, in shopkeepers' slang, "ate the profits."

To newcomers from Anglo-Saxon countries in the early twentieth century, Montparnasse was a revelation. In their repressed societies, no respectable man would be seen in public except in a three-piece suit and a collar and tie; a woman appearing at night without a hat was practically advertising herself as a whore, while, as Cole Porter noted, "a glimpse of stocking / Was looked on as something shocking."

The height of revolt for an American woman, however, was to cut, or "bob," her hair. In Scott Fitzgerald's story "Bernice Bobs Her Hair," the unpopular Bernice hints she's thinking of having her hair cut, and might, under the right circumstances, allow some boy to be present when she does, a provocation as inflammatory in today's terms as inviting him to watch her take a shower. And yet in Paris, the *garçonne* boy/girl look was all the rage, with some women not only cutting their hair as short as a man's but also abandoning skirts altogether for male trousers and jackets.

Since, in polite Anglo-Saxon society, one spoke only to people to whom one had been introduced, and even then exchanged only the most banal of pleasantries, it amused the French to see the enthusiasm with which new arrivals embraced social freedoms Europeans took for granted. "What appealed to them," wrote Michel Georges-Michel in his 1929 novel *Les Montparnos*, "was this moral liberty which they knew neither in London nor in any city of free and austere America; the international *kermesse* [carnival] of the Rotonde, the Dôme, the Parnasse, where, indiscriminately and at any hour, even on Sunday, they could work, drink, play the piano, and dance *even with girls they did not know*."

Fitzgerald wrote in *The Great Gatsby* that visitors to Gatsby's mansion arrived at his parties uninvited, and thereafter "conducted themselves according to the rules of behavior associated with amusement parks." Tourists came to Montparnasse in the same spirit. Seeing men dining publicly with their mistresses and artists with their models, prostitutes trolling for business, blacks, Asians, and whites mixing in sexual and social equality, alcohol and drugs openly available, homosexuality freely practiced by both women and men, they imagined that the French obeyed no moral code at all.

In fact, the French were as conservative as the stuffiest Bostonian, but about totally different things. Respect for their cultural heritage and the French language, for the soil of their ancestors, and above all for family ties united them on a level that visitors seldom sensed. Bohemians might misbehave in the cafés, but in nearby rooming houses eagle-eyed concierges kept unmarried tenants apart, while nosy neighbors could ruin a girl's reputation and hopes of marriage.

Much as they welcomed the influx of foreign money, the French regarded the newcomers as less a blessing than a blight, and their arrogance as an offence. With the franc worth almost nothing, some tourists, emerging drunkenly from the cafés, threw their change onto the sidewalk as one might toss coins to street kids. The Montparnos seethed, but scrambled for it anyway. Almost worthless to Americans, a few francs could buy bread, even pay the rent.

André Breton lived in Montparnasse after World War I until, disgusted by its triviality, he moved to Montmartre. To discourage the Surrealists from wasting their time in his former neighborhood he insisted they meet with him every night at the Cyrano on Place Blanche in the ninth *arrondissement*, on the far side of the city. As it turned out, things were not much better there. "I've been living for two months on Place Blanche," he wrote. "Women make brief but charming appearances on the café *terrasse*, which seems to be a favorite for drug dealers."

To the new arrivals from America, the rudeness and indiscipline of Montparnasse signified authenticity. Jimmie Charters, barman at the Dingo, one of the most popular expatriate bars, wrote of arriving one evening almost at the same time as Florence "Flossie" Martin, a former Broadway showgirl notorious for her profane dislike of tourists.

> As she came abreast of the bar entrance, a handsome Rolls Royce drove up to the curb and from it stepped two lavishly dressed ladies. For a moment they hesitated. They looked at the Dingo questioningly. They peered in the windows between the curtains.

Flossie, seeing them, looked her contempt. As she passed into the bar she tossed a single phrase over her shoulder.

"You bitch!"

Whereupon the lady so addressed nudged her companion anxiously.

"Come on, Helen," she said. "This must be the place!"

Until 1927, when the spacious La Coupole opened, with its afternoon tea dances, cocktail bar, and downstairs ballroom where the band played until four a.m., most Americans congregated at the Dôme. A cab driver stuck with an Anglo tourist too drunk or confused to remember the address of his hotel would dump him there, confident someone would see him home. Generally the new arrival just got even drunker. A 1929 vignette in *The New Yorker* gave a vivid snapshot of a typical night.

The Dôme blossoms like some impossible mushroom. Tables huddle together in a vast mélange and spill into the street, where the shifting mob laugh, whistle, gesticulate, consume vast quantities of aperitifs and liqueurs, and vociferously absolve themselves of America.

It's not true that the Dôme is solely occupied by transatlantic wastrels and pretenders. There are ambitious young poets here, aspiring musicians, intense experimenters in creative prose. Why they are here is unexplainable. The Dôme offers nothing but a churning oasis of the Left Bank where Americans may see one another and, gratified with the spectacle of kindred blood in a foreign land, succumb to the delectable illusion that they are liberated.

Foreign celebrities who might have been expected to set a good example often behaved worse than anyone. Isadora Duncan partied, as she danced, with the passion of Salome and in just as little clothing. Describing one of her soirées, Michel Georges-Michel wrote, "Isadora, reclining on a couch, Roman fashion, poured out champagne from an immense amphora of jade to all those who reached up with their cups. She had let down her hair, opened her veils and asked everybody to follow her example. 'It is as indecent to be dressed when the company is nude as to be sober when everybody is drunk.'"

Novelist Ford Madox Ford also liked to party, but, according to the *Times of London* correspondent Sisley Huddleston, "extended his invitations at random. The result was that the most nondescript crowd appeared. There was plenty of drink, to which the unknown guests helped themselves. When they had drunk too much, they would fight." After a few such brawls had wrecked his home, Ford moved his parties to a *bal musette*. "It was in a working-class district," wrote Huddleston, "and the habitual dancers were astonished at this strange apparition of artists and writers and hangers-on." But as long as the foreigners got drunk together and only fought among themselves, the locals just shrugged and danced on.

Café de Flore.

CAFÉ DE FLORE,
BOULEVARD SAINT-GERMAIN

That the Dôme had no equivalent in Saint-Germain highlights the difference between the two districts. Montparnasse cafés catered to tourists who came there to party, generally at night. In Saint-Germain, the cafés' regular patrons were French and spent most of their day there, particularly since, being musicians, actors, prostitutes, writers, and artists, they had no regular work.

The Café de Flore (pronounced *Flow*) was the favorite of Jean-Paul Sartre, his companion Simone de Beauvoir, their friend Albert Camus, and the trio's numerous admirers. "We are completely settled there," Sartre explained. "From nine o'clock in the morning until midday, we work, then we eat, and at two o'clock we come back and chat with friends until eight o'clock. After dinner, we see people who have an appointment. That may seem strange to you, but we are at home at the Flore."

Avoiding both the main café, with its tiled floor and red upholstered banquettes, and the glassed-in *terrasse* looking out on boulevard Saint-Germain,

Sartre and his group preferred the large room on the first floor where generations of other intellectuals had talked and worked.

Of Saint-Germain's few surviving literary cafés, only the Flore retains an atmosphere of the private club, sadly combined today with an arrogance and snobbery that the management of such establishments regards as essential. Paradoxically, it's in the branches of the ubiquitous Starbucks that the simpler tradition of impoverished writers working all day in a café survives closest to its original form. Laptops replace notebooks, and the *café crème* and *fine à l'eau* are supplanted by the Hot Wet Skinny Venti Frappuccino.

A handful of literary groups and individuals still make the Flore their informal headquarters. And though they may lack the stature of Henry Miller, some expatriate *flâneurs* can be found on the *terrasse* at weekends, lionized by blue-rinsed ladies from the Midwest while their husbands frown at the *addition*, unable to believe how much they're being charged for a few cups of coffee.

To experience the Flore in something like its original form, take a table at the edge of the *terrasse* one afternoon, almost around the corner on rue Saint-Benoit, order an express and a glass of water, and just spend an hour watching people. You won't be disappointed. And maybe you'll glimpse the ghost of Sartre. He drops by sometimes, late in the day, but, after one frowning glance at the clientele, the prices, and the autocratic direction, doesn't linger.

Simone de Beauvoir at Jean-Paul Sartre's funeral, 1980.

4

GOD AND GUNPOWDER

Fear God, and keep his commandments: for this is the
whole duty of man.
THE BIBLE, KING JAMES VERSION,
ECCLESIASTES 12:13

WHERE COMMUNITIES IN OTHER COUNTRIES GREW UP around a trading post, a military fort, a river crossing, or a coaching inn, French towns began with a church. Scores of them remain embedded in Paris. At one time, each was surrounded by a cluster of other buildings and a graveyard, the "hallowed ground" denied to suicides. Today only the churches survive, like the hard seeds of fruit from which the flesh has been gnawed.

Traditionally, the church dominated Saint-Germain. To its early abbots and bishops, the land on the southern slope of the Left Bank seemed to have been put there with them in mind. Avoiding the swampy river meadows, they built on higher ground, in the *prés*, or fields. By the seventeenth century, the largest abbey, Saint-Germain-des-Prés, owned everything on that side of the Seine.

Throughout the Dark Ages, the churches conserved civilization. Within their walls, scholars pursued medicine, philosophy, and the arts. At a time when aristocracy took little interest in the peasantry, the church supplied what we call the social services: education, health care, aid for the poor and helpless. For young men of ambition, only two avenues existed for improvement, the army and the church, the choice between military red and ecclesiastical black, which Stendhal dramatized in his novel *Le Rouge et le Noir*.

Next to the larger abbeys, orders of nuns opened schools. A guesthouse accommodated visiting monks, the "peripatetics" who roamed Europe, studying at the scriptoria or libraries which contained the few precious hand-copied texts, all that survived of ancient wisdom. Monks cultivated farms, vineyards, and orchards. Distilleries created both herbal medicines and infusions of herbs in alcohol that supposedly encouraged appetite or aided digestion. These aperitifs and digestifs become the standard tipples of the French, the backbone of café drinking.

The Abbey of Saint-Germain-des-Prés, founded in the sixth century by Benedictine monks, led by the Abbot (later Saint) Germain, was the largest on the Left Bank.

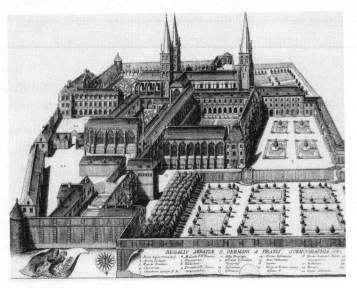

The Abbey of St. Germain-des-Prés, 13th century.

More castle than church, it had high stone walls and a water-filled moat. One entered through an imposing gate facing the Gothic church.

For the peasantry, the tolling of the church's bells parsed their day. As well as marking the hours, they emphasized who owned their land and labor. At noon, as the Angelus chimed, all put aside their scythe or plow, bowed their heads, and prayed.

The revolution of 1789 violently terminated ecclesiastical power. Venting the accumulated hatred of centuries, those peasants ripped up vineyards and orchards, looted granaries, and built houses on what had been holy ground. Priests, monks, and nuns were slaughtered after rumors spread that Italy was raising an army to rescue fellow Catholics.

Under a state-endorsed belief system, churches were forced to replace images of Christ with the slogan "The French people recognize the Supreme Being and the Immortality of the Soul." The cathedral of Notre Dame became a warehouse, the church of Saint-Sulpice a hall for meetings, and the ancient church of Saint-Germain a factory to make gunpowder. In 1803, the store of saltpeter exploded, demolishing most of the church and the other buildings around it.

Over the next century, peasants abandoned the land for manufacturing and trade. Houses invaded the fields. Saint-Germain became a suburb. All that remained of the abbey was the church itself. Several attempts at repair left it a muddle of architectural styles, but the building still stood. Lapped on every side by self-indulgence, atheism, and vice, it was determined, like the religion it represented, to survive.

"I need someone to photograph the Saint-Germain church," I told my daughter, Louise. "Do you feel like going with me?"

Actually I didn't really need photographs so much as

company. Brought up a Catholic, I retain enough belief
to feel uncomfortable on holy ground. The English poet
Philip Larkin experienced the same uneasiness. In his
poem "Church Going," he noticed how visiting a church,
whether or not one was a believer, encouraged reflections
on life and death. He believed churches would never entirely disappear . . .

> *Since someone will forever be surprising*
> *A hunger in himself to be more serious,*
> *And gravitating with it to this ground,*
> *Which, he once heard, was proper to grow wise in,*
> *If only that so many dead lie round.*

"I don't mind," Louise said.

Of the church's tradition of learning, education, and
charity, there's little sign these days unless you count some
brochures in the vestibule appealing for funds to restore the
building, and a single beggar installed just outside the main
door. He's brought a cushion to insulate his butt from the
chill stone. A card with the bleak message "SDF"—*Sans
Domicile Fixe*, i.e., homeless—is propped next to the ubiquitous Styrofoam cup.

Louise's generation grew up on Catholicism Lite. Hell
to them was an abstraction, not the imminent reality it had

been to me as a child. Confession had devolved into a sort of group therapy—sin not so much condemned as frowned on, like bad breath.

On this overcast Monday morning, the only signs of life inside the church are a few candles, their flames barely wavering in the still air. Though a card with photographs of half a dozen cheery faces assures us these priests are available to hear confessions, a padlock secures the sacristy door, and the dusty wooden confessionals gape like empty sentry boxes at some provincial château whose gates have long since rusted open.

"You'll want this, I expect," Louise says, raising her camera to shoot the back wall of a tiny chapel where three discreet black panels with inscriptions in Latin identify the dignitaries whose remains are walled up there.

One is René Descartes, the seventeenth-century thinker often credited as the father of philosophy. About him, I could scratch up the usual Trivial Pursuit factoids: his statement *"Cogito ergo sum"* ("I think, therefore I am") and the odd circumstances of his death. Queen Christina of Sweden—the one Greta Garbo played on screen—summoned him to give her lessons on the latest in intellectual thought, but insisted on starting at five a.m. Her castle's icy corridors were too much for Descartes, who died of pneumonia. The Swedes repatriated his body to the friendlier surroundings of Saint-Germain. His skull and a finger were lost in the mail, but the rest of him lies here behind a sleek black panel, gold-lettered in Latin.

But my favorite occupant of the Saint-Germain church is Lord James Douglas, one of the many Scots who preferred to fight for Catholic France rather than bow to the Protestant English. When he died in 1645, Louis XIII accorded him a lavish tomb. His life-size effigy reclines on top of it, in full uniform, including sword, but with one unexpected addition. Suspecting that there won't be much to do in the afterlife, Douglas has brought a book.

"Ah," said Louise, raising her camera and focusing

Tomb of James Douglas, church of Saint Germain-des-Prés.

on that detail. "So this is what you *really* want." She starts snapping busily. "What's the title?"

I'd already checked the book's marble cover. It's blank. Perhaps it's the journal of what must have been an eventful life. As Oscar Wilde said, "I never travel without my diary. One should always have something sensational to read in the train." How much more appropriate then to take one on this, the longest journey of all.

THE CHURCH OF
SAINT-GERMAIN-DES-PRÉS

The church is best approached from the rear, along rue de l'Abbaye, these days lined by smart shops selling upholstery fabric. One showroom preserves a few meters of wall from a thirteenth-century chapel flattened by the 1803 explosion.

From rue de l'Abbaye, it's easy to see the damage. A couple of flying buttresses support what remains of the original, but halfway down the length of the building, the texture of the brickwork changes, and the pointed Gothic windows give way to rounded Romanesque.

Of the fields that gave the abbey its name, nothing survives. Where the gate stood, there's a wide cobbled square. Opposite are the café Les Deux Magots and a shop selling the fashionable luggage of Louis Vuitton.

In common with most older French churches, the pulpit of Saint-Germain-des-Prés occupies the center of the building. Instead of pews, there are low stiff-backed chairs, with seats of woven sea grass. Most days, a few silent men, hands clasped, eyes lowered, occupy a couple of them. Other worshippers kneel on the cold stone floor. They are outnumbered by tourists, mostly Japanese, who wander the long side aisles, peering into little chapels, giving serious attention to the stained glass, far gaudier than the abstract windows of Notre Dame.

The memorials to Descartes and James Douglas are on the right as you walk in. Circle round under the slim marble columns that survive from the original interior, and you'll find the lavish tomb of King Casimir of Poland, who became abbot in 1669. He's shown offering his crown and scepter to God.

5

RIMBAUD'S POLICEMAN

One must be a living man and a posthumous artist.
JEAN COCTEAU

A MODEST CHAPEL TO THE VIRGIN ONCE STOOD NEXT TO
the church of Saint-Germain-des-Prés. Having survived
since the thirteenth century and endured being used as
a grain storehouse after the revolution, it was reduced to
rubble by the 1803 explosion that demolished most of the
church. So little remained that it wasn't worth rebuilding.
Locals used the stones to strengthen their houses, leaving
only the frames of some Gothic windows, which are now
attached to the church wall.

After lying derelict for more than a century, the park
was cleaned up in the 1950s and dedicated to the poet and
critic Wilhelm Albert Vladimir Apollinaris Kostrowitzky,
better known as Guillaume Apollinaire.

Overweight, dour, and darkly witty, Apollinaire

prowled Saint-Germain before World War I, spending much of his time at the Café de Flore, where he wrote his columns for the magazine *Mercure de France*, crafted the clever graphics he called *calligrammes*, and coined the word "surreal" to describe the games with the unconscious played by André Breton and his friends.

Bisexual, iconoclastic, and intimately acquainted with the underworld, Apollinaire also took a keen interest in pornography. As well as scholarly introductions to new editions of classic erotica, he wrote two novels, the auto-biographical *Les Exploits d'un Jeune Don Juan* (*Exploits of a Young Don Juan*) and an unflinchingly anatomical tale about a priapic Romanian military officer, set during the Russo-Japanese war of 1904–5. Published anonymously as *Les Onze Mille Verges*, literally *The Eleven Thousand Rods*, it sold better under its English title *The Debauched Hospodar*.

Apollinaire and Pablo Picasso had been friends and allies. When Cubism was battling for acceptance, Apollinaire defended it. One of his underworld acquaintances, a petty thief named Géry Pieret, occasionally sneaked some treasures out of the Louvre's crowded storerooms. No fan of the Louvre, Apollinaire, who'd suggested burning it down as a gesture against the establishment, fenced Pieret's loot to friends. Picasso bought some ancient stone heads carved in post-Roman Spain. Echoes of them appear in his most ambitious work of the time, *Les Demoiselles d'Avignon*.

Pieret's thefts might have gone undiscovered had not the *Mona Lisa* disappeared in August 1911. When a newspaper offered a reward for information, Pieret foolishly applied, producing one of the stolen heads as proof of the Louvre's lax security. Interrogated, he implicated Apollinaire and Picasso, who were hauled in for questioning. The police released Picasso, but Apollinaire spent a week in jail and wasn't exonerated until *La Gioconda* surfaced in Italy two years later.

Weakened from a head wound contracted in the trenches, Apollinaire died of influenza during the 1920 epidemic, aged only thirty-eight. In the 1950s, the authorities of the sixth *arrondissement* began belatedly to celebrate its cultural heroes. Though his former home at 202 boulevard Saint-Germain already bore a plaque, they decided Apollinaire deserved a monument, and chose the vacant lot next to the church as the site.

Picasso offered to contribute a bust, but bridled when the council chose to look this substantial gift horse in the mouth. Some councilors disliked his art; others objected to his recently joining the Communist Party They asked to see some sketches. Insulted, Picasso refused, so they dedicated the park instead to Laurent-Désiré Prache, a pre–

World War I civil servant whose greatest achievement was bringing gas to the city's kitchens.

But supporters of an Apollinaire memorial persisted, and in 1959 got their way. Picasso, however, was no longer willing to create a new bust. Grudgingly he offered one he'd completed in 1941—not of Apollinaire, however, but of Picasso's former mistress Dora Maar. As it existed only in plaster, the council would also have to finance a cast in bronze. Even so, they voted to accept it. To get around the fact that the bust didn't depict Apollinaire at all, someone suggested the park be dedicated not to him specifically but to "Poetry." That Maar was a photographer, not a poet, was brushed aside as a minor detail.

The Surrealist in Apollinaire would probably have appreciated the inconsistencies of his monument. Inaugurated in June 1959, it stood in a park dedicated to someone else while memorializing another with a bust of a third—who, in addition to being a woman, had never even met Apollinaire.

To speak at the unveiling, the council invited seventy-year-old Jean Cocteau, one of the poet's oldest friends. Some women at the 1917 premiere of the ballet *Parade* had been so enraged by Erik Satie's jazz score, Picasso's Cubist costumes, and Cocteau's puzzling script that they'd advanced on its author, armed with needle-sharp hat pins. "If it had not been for Apollinaire in uniform," Cocteau wrote, "with his skull shaved, the scar on his temple and the bandage around his head, the women would have gouged our eyes out."

Painter, poet, filmmaker, novelist, playwright, and musician, Cocteau was above all an inspired self-publicist with an instinct for the limelight. Notorious at the time for his homosexuality and opium addiction—at one point, he smoked sixty pipes a day—he moved effortlessly, as Apollinaire had done, between the worlds of high and low art, writing libretti for operas and ballet but also managing the career of tap-dancing boxer "Panama" Al Brown and playing drums at the jazz club Le Boeuf sur le Toit (The Ox on the Roof), which he cofounded.

Neither existentialist nor Surrealist, fascist nor communist, Catholic nor atheist, he'd flirted at some time with all of them. Grieving over the death of his lover, young novelist Raymond Radiguet, he briefly converted to the neo-Catholic cult of Jacques Maritain, only to switch his allegiance to the fascist Front Nationale. During the occupation, he joined other celebrities such as Coco Chanel and Maurice Chevalier in cozying up to the Nazis.

For almost ten years, he'd been the semipermanent houseguest of millionairess Francine Weisweiller at her villa on the Côte d'Azur. When not decorating chapels and public buildings along the Riviera, his life passed in an atmosphere of self-indulgence, opium, and the company of husky young fishermen who visited the villa, ostensibly to model.

André Breton detested all homosexuals but loathed Cocteau in particular for his readiness to follow political and social fashion. Cocteau in turn mocked Breton's autocratic manner. He'd called him a "Rimbaud gendarme" (a Rimbaud policeman) who had appointed himself custodian of such poets as Arthur Rimbaud and felt entitled to lay down the law about them. That Breton's father had been a gendarme added sting to the insult.

Cocteau agreed to attend the unveiling. That's when the trouble started.

Apollinaire monument by Picasso, Saint Germain-des-Prés.

Jean Cocteau at work on a mural in Villefranche-sur-mer, 1957.

MEMORIAL TO GUILLAUME APOLLINAIRE,
PARC DU LAURENT-DÉSIRÉ PRACHE

The crowd that gathered for the unveiling of Apollinaire's memorial should have warned of trouble ahead. Picasso didn't attend. Neither did Dora Maar. Breton came, however, with the widow of painter Francis Picabia and with Tristan Tzara, whose Dada movement foreshadowed surrealism.

Cocteau, pale and thin, with the translucent, faintly yellow skin of the *opiomane*, appeared almost ethereal as he started to read his deeply personal and poetic eulogy. "It was not given to Guillaume Apollinaire to reign in the sky of letters," he began, only to be heckled by Breton, Tzara, and their supporters. Ignoring them, he continued in praise of his old friend.

He preferred to botanize at the edge of the Seine and at the edge of the Rhine. He did not believe in his glory, and died without realizing that his face, flanked by wax candles, would resemble the severed head of Orpheus, that its war wound prefigured his star, that on November 11th the city would put out flags in its honor, and that

the muses would lovingly choose him, as praying
mantises devour those whom they wed.

As admirers clustered around to congratulate Cocteau and the Breton group departed, satisfied it had made its point, commentators mourned the longevity of feuds in this most argumentative culture. "Breton harbored a need to hate Cocteau," noted one. "The era of *Boeuf sur le Toit*, the Maritain period, the mobs of *Front National*, the years of the Occupation, the cellars of Saint-Germain-des-Prés—these belonged to history, but '*Rimbaud gendarme*' continued to wave his stick."

The drama wasn't over yet. In April 1999, the bust disappeared. Police blamed friends of Dora Maar. She'd died in 1997, still maligning Picasso, who had treated her as badly as he did all his lovers. After four years, it was recovered and reerected.

Today, the little park is still named for Laurent-Désiré Prache, a plaster relief of whom is attached to the church wall. Recently a memorial was added commemorating those Jewish children of Saint-Germain, including an eight-month-old baby, who, with the connivance of the French police, were deported to die in Germany during World War II.

The bust remains, but on a plinth that gives Apollinaire's name and the dates of his birth and death. Nothing indicates that the artist was Picasso, nor that Maar is the subject. Most visitors leave with the impression that Apollinaire was an effeminate-looking man with an odd taste in haircuts. As a Surrealist, he would have been amused.

6

A GOOD READ

Enter Hamlet, reading.
Lord Polonius: What do you read, my lord?
Hamlet: Words, words, words.
WILLIAM SHAKESPEARE, *HAMLET*

JUST INSIDE THE NORTHERN GATE OF THE JARDIN DU LUXEM-bourg, half hidden by trees, the bust of a nineteenth-century gentleman in beard, mustache, formal suit, and cravat perches on a column. A garland of stone roses straggles around his chest and trails down the plinth, an attempt by the sculptor to soften his grim expression. It fails. The subject resembles a college president entangled in some student prank. The roses haven't fooled him. Next comes a pie in the face.

Considering he almost single-handedly inspired the myth of bohemian Paris, Henry Murger should look happier. But he never lived to enjoy his fame. His *Scènes de la Vie de Bohème* (*Scenes of Bohemian Life*), first collected as a book in 1851, when he was only twenty-seven, would be his only success. He died penniless, aged only thirty-eight. It wasn't until 1896 that Giacomo Puccini transformed his tales into the immensely popular opera *La Bohème* and made their author famous.

For all its romanticizing, *La Bohème* captures the essence of nineteenth-century student life, since Murger took most of its incidents from his own experience. The hotel in the Latin Quarter shared by my girlfriend and me during our first Paris visit could once have been the rooming house where Rodolfo and his friends lived. Before central heating, one could understand them burning their manuscripts to keep warm. As for Mimi, his lover, seamstresses like her were commonplace, many of them suffering, as she does, from "consumption," i.e., tuberculosis, which, as the name implies, ate their flesh down to the bone.

Often too poor to afford wine, Rodolfo and his friends call themselves "the water drinkers." For warmth and company, they hang out in cafés, arguing, loafing, always hoping someone will buy them a drink. But Murger saw a reverse snobbery in their behavior. "They find in bohemian life an existence full of seductions," he wrote.

> *Not to eat every day, to sleep in the open on wet nights, and to dress in nankeen [light cotton] in*

the month of December seems to them the paradise of human felicity. They suddenly turn their backs upon an honorable future to seek the adventure of a hazardous career. But as the most robust cannot stand a mode of living that would render Hercules consumptive, they soon give up the game, and, hastening back to the paternal Sunday roast dinner, marry their little cousins, set up as a notary in a town of thirty thousand inhabitants, and by their fireside of an evening have the satisfaction of relating their artistic misery with the magniloquence of a traveler narrating a tiger hunt.

When Murger's characters are down to their last sou, they head for the nearest bookshop—not to buy but to sell. That too is a Saint-Germain tradition, at its busiest along boulevard Saint-Michel.

Gibert Joseph is the biggest bookshop in Paris, perhaps even in France. Not a single store but a community of them, it has departments scattered along boulevard Saint-Michel: one for textbooks, another for art supplies and stationery, a third for books on travel, another for school textbooks, culminating in the flagship store, six floors of crowded shelves arranged in a labyrinthine system that only the staff fully understand.

One policy in particular singles Gibert out from other French bookshops, and has created a culture all its own. It buys clean copies of used books and shelves them next to newer editions—a useful amenity for cash-poor students and one reason it has stayed afloat while more selective shops closed their doors.

There is usually a long line at its buying department on rue Pierre Sarrazin, a side street next to the main shop. Selling is simple. At the counter, a scanner reads the bar code. If it's not a popular title or they already have too many copies, you're out of luck.

Occasionally we load some bags with discards and

Selling books at Gibert.

haul them there. The first time I did so, a young North African man darted across the street and murmured in my ear.

"What they don't take," he said, "you give me, OK?"

He returned to his group. All were Arab or African. Each guarded a few book-filled cartons. Occasionally one would spot someone else sweating up the hill with loaded shopping bags and sprint across to make the same offer.

As I exited with my unsold books, the young African was at my side.

"I take, OK?"

He emptied my discards into a carton. And after that? Wherever they ended up, I was relieved of the guilt of dumping them in the garbage.

There's a long tradition of these subcultures in Saint-Germain. Back in the nineteenth century, the pickpockets would meet every morning on Place Saint-Michel. Depending on what was happening that day—a race at Longchamp, an exhibition opening at the Grand Palais—they'd be sent to whichever offered the best pickings.

Mention of pickpockets sent me into my copy of Émile Gaboriau's *Monsieur Lecoq*, a novel featuring ace detective Vidocq. The petty thieves of Gaboriau's Paris weren't too different from modern-day book runners.

After midnight, these gloomy, narrow streets became the haunt of numerous homeless vagabonds, and escaped criminals and malefactors, moreover, made the quarter their rendezvous. If the day had been a lucky one, they made merry over their spoils, and when sleep overtook them, hid in doorways or among the rubbish in deserted houses.

The scavengers on rue Pierre Sarrazin would never look quite the same to me again.

Jim Carroll, proprietor of The San Francisco Book Company.

THE SAN FRANCISCO BOOK COMPANY,
17 RUE MONSIEUR LE PRINCE

So what *does* happen to the books collected on rue Pierre Sarrazin? I decided to ask the man who, on any matter concerning books in Saint-Germain, was the guru.

To call Jim Carroll a dealer in secondhand books is like describing Michelangelo, on the basis of the Sistine Chapel, as a house painter.

For the visitor in search of information and education, a visit to his San Francisco Book Company is an essential part of the Paris experience.

A native of Nebraska, Jim brings a Gary Cooper reticence and good sense to the often bizarre world of print. His arrival in Saint-Germain in 1997 after years as a bookseller in San Francisco was the harbinger of the area's revival as a haven for bibliophiles. Shops specializing in rare books have since sprung up on nearby rue Gregoire de Tours, rue Casimir Delavigne, and even on rue de l'Odéon, site of Sylvia Beach's original Shakespeare and Company.

The San Francisco Book Company maintains the area's expatriate literary tradition in its most effective form: by preserving its products. Behind Jim's desk, a glass cabinet holds a treasury of rare first editions, while in long corridors the wealth of literature lies in wait for the inquisitive mind. I've often turned to browse a shelf while waiting for Jim to close a sale, only to emerge an hour later from the depths of the store, arms piled with seductive obscurities. Anthony Powell called one of his novels *Books Do Furnish a Room*. One can equally say they furnish a mind.

And the runners of rue Pierre Sarrazin?

"They come in," says Jim. "Occasionally I buy a few things—though sometimes what they offer is the same unsalable books I put in my giveaway box outside the shop a few days back. But booksellers have to buy—otherwise what would they sell? Like Arthur Miller said, 'It comes with the territory.'"

7

THE SWEETEST SIN

> *The mingled scents of chocolate, vanilla, heated copper*
> *and cinnamon are intoxicating, powerfully suggestive;*
> *the raw and earthy tang of the Americas, the hot and res-*
> *inous perfume of the rainforest. This is how I travel now,*
> *as the Aztecs did in their sacred rituals. Mexico, Vene-*
> *zuela, Colombia. The court of Montezuma. Cortez and*
> *Columbus. The food of the gods, bubbling and frothing*
> *in ceremonial goblets. The bitter elixir of life.*
>
> JOANNE HARRIS, *CHOCOLAT*

TWO FLAVORS INSINUATE THEMSELVES MORE DEEPLY INTO our sensorium than any other, gratifying senses that other materials barely tickle. One is bacon. But the dark prince of them all is chocolate.

Not only does it taste delicious. It's also good for you. Or so believed the German chemist Justus von Liebig, who pioneered the canning and preserving of food, and has the dubious distinction of inventing the stock cube. He praised chocolate as "a perfect food, as wholesome as it is delicious, a beneficent restorer of exhausted power." To the enduring satisfaction of every writer with a sweet tooth, he also called it "the best friend of those engaged in literary pursuits."

Some artists have gone further in promoting chocolate's therapeutic properties. In Joanne Harris's novel *Chocolat*, later a successful film, a wandering chocolatier and her daughter open a shop in a small French town and humanize the locals with their products.

Creating a drink from the cocoa pod is even more difficult than processing tea leaves or coffee beans. To become edible, the beans must be dried, fermented, and refined to remove their bitterness. Only then can they become chocolate liquor or cocoa butter, which in turn is cast in slabs, ground to powder, and mixed with water and sugar to become the drink we know today.

When it arrived in Europe from Mexico in the middle of the seventeenth century, people took chocolate less for pleasure than as medicine. Early descriptions classified it as a drug. Physicians of the 1650s recommended it for "vapors of the spleen." In 1823, Antoine Gallais claimed chocolate was "prescribed by doctors with great success in cases of colds, catarrh, angina and those irritations of the throat which have become so frequent at this time because of the continual changes in the atmosphere. Chocolate also makes the organs of breathing more supple, helps those recovering from gastritis, and from all afflictions caused by inflammation."

Others were not so convinced of its benign effects. The Marquise de Sévigné, a lady at the court of Louis XIV and a tireless letter writer, liked hot chocolate so well that her young African servant brought her a pot in bed each morning and evening. She cut back as rumors circulated of dangerous side effects. "But what do you have to say about chocolate?" she wrote to her pregnant daughter in 1671.

Are you not afraid of how it can burn the blood? What if all the effects that appear miraculous mask some sort of diabolical combustion? What do your doctors say? I loved chocolate, as you know. But I think it did burn me; and furthermore, I have heard many terrible stories about it. The Marquise de Coëtlogon drank so much chocolate when she was pregnant last year that she gave birth to a baby who was black as the devil, and died.

Chocolate came to England from France. In 1657, the London *Public Advertiser* advertised that "in Bishopgate Street, in Queen's Head Alley, at a Frenchman's house, is an excellent West Indian drink called chocolate, to be sold, where you may have it ready at any time, or unmade, at reasonable rates." Liebig may have made chocolate respectable, but the French—and specifically Marie Antoinette, wife of King Louis XVI—made it fashionable. In 1790, she asked her court pharmacist, Sulpice Debauve, if he could make more palatable the powdered medicine prescribed by her doctors. Blending the drug with cocoa, sugar, and almond milk, Debauve cast the mixture in discs that resembled a Spanish gold coin, the pistole. In a final touch, he embossed each in gold with the royal emblem, the origin of today's foil-wrapped chocolates.

Not only the queen but also other ladies of the court found these sweet little jewels irresistible. Little has changed over the centuries since. In Alfred Hitchcock's film *North by Northwest*, Cary Grant tells his secretary to send chocolates to a girlfriend: "You know the kind—each piece wrapped in gold paper. She'll like that. She'll think she's eating money."

In transforming what had been a beverage into something solid and portable, Debauve created more than a confection. It permeates the modern diet, from a bowl of chocolate breakfast cereal to the after-dinner mint. Even war can't curtail our craving. Every serviceman's survival kit contains a chocolate bar. During World War I, one French manufacturer insensitively marketed a range of combat-related confectionery, including a chocolate facsimile of France's highest military honor, the Croix de Guerre, and even a 75mm artillery shell, the explosive replaced with chocolate.

Chocolatiers of distinction are scattered across Paris. There's a simple reason, rooted, like so much in French society, in the question of manners.

Since an invitation to visit someone's home is a matter of some formality, it's usual to take a small gift. However, to bring anything that the hosts might be expected to provide themselves—wine, for example, or any kind of food—might be seen as a slur on their hospitality. Imagine someone turning up for dinner at your house bringing his and her own cutlery, on the assumption that yours would not be good enough.

Over centuries, the range of appropriate gifts has narrowed. The easiest option is flowers, particularly from a fashionable florist. *Which* florist can matter a great deal, and provident hostesses sometimes save the wrapping paper of a particularly chic one for later use on bouquets bought somewhere less expensive.

Although the warning against bringing cakes remains, there's recently been a fashion for *macarons*, those tiny multicolored gateaux that hover somewhere between cookie and bonbon. Again, provenance matters. When innovative young patissier Pierre Hermé flavored his Ispahan with fresh raspberries and topped each with a real red rose petal, the long-established Ladurée responded with a black *macaron* made with licorice, for which the French have a special liking. A dozen of these in one of Ladurée's colorful floral boxes trumps almost everything else. Except, of course, chocolate.

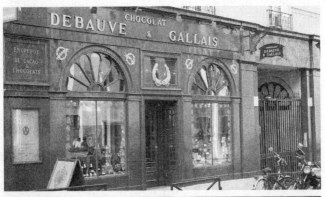

Debauve et Gallais's original shop.

DEBAUVE ET GALLAIS, CHOCOLATIERS,
30 RUE DES SAINTS-PÈRES

As the first chocolate to reach France was reserved for royalty, it never lost its aura of luxury and exclusivity. Shrewd chocolatiers emphasized this connection in naming their stores. One chain adopted the name of the Marquise de Sévigné. Another company, acknowledging that Belgium and the Netherlands have done more than most nations to refine chocolate manufacture, borrowed the name of Belgium's most scenic medieval city, calling itself Jeff de Bruges.

More exclusive than either, however, is Debauve et Gallais. Luckier than his former employers, court pharmacist Sulpice Debauve survived the revolution of 1789 and launched his first shop in 1800. His nephew Antoine Gallais joined him in 1823.

Until the late eighteenth century, shops as we know them didn't exist. A merchant simply opened his front door and clients walked in off the street. However, by 1835, one admiring journalist could write of Paris merchants, "*Charcutiers, patissiers* and bakers distinguish themselves among the pro-

Tour de Nesle.

fessions by the beauty of the *decors* that ornament their businesses, which are for the most part gilding on glass or paintings on canvas placed under glass to create the best effect possible."

As chocolatier to the court of Napoleon, Debauve had the emperor's architects, Charles Percier and Pierre Fontaine, design his premises. A gem of the Empire style, the shop suited a city that was coming to see itself as an imperial capital to rival ancient Athens or Rome. A circle of slim columns supports the interior, their capitals decorated with the traditional acanthus-leaf motif, while the distinctive blue-and-gray boxes, embossed in gold and reserved for royalty until 1913, display a fleur-de-lis, the stylized lily of the Bourbon kings. The design is in use to this day, making a box of Debauve et Gallais pistoles, invented for Marie Antoinette, a gift no person would forget.

8

HIGH CRIMES AND MISDEMEANORS

The pretty girl who slept with the king of Prussia
With the king of Prussia.
They shaved her head completely bald
Her head completely bald.

GEORGE BRASSENS, "THE SHAVED GIRL"

"I DO NOT KNOW MUCH ABOUT GODS," T. S. ELIOT WROTE, "but I think that the river is a strong brown god—sullen, untamed and intractable." Parisians look on the Seine with similar respect. So vital is the river that all streets, not only those in Saint-Germain but throughout the city, are numbered from its banks. The lower a street number, the closer it is to the Seine.

Few of the medieval buildings that fringed the Left Bank survive except in legend. The most lurid stories cluster round the Hôtel de Nesle (pronounced *Nel*) and the ninety-foot tower, the Tour de Nesle, that once overhung the dark, fast-flowing waters.

In 1314, France was ruled of Philip IV, known as Philip le Bel, or Philip the Handsome. Notoriously unemotional, preoccupied with protecting France's good name, he was, remarked one of his retinue, "neither a man nor a beast but a statue." To bolster his claim to Burgundy, contested by the British, Philip married off his three sons, Louis, Philip, and Charles, to the daughters of Burgundian nobles, and his one daughter, Isabella, nicknamed "the iron virago," to Edward II of England. (Openly gay, Edward would be assassinated in 1327. As it was treason to draw a sword in the royal presence, his killers forced a red-hot poker up his rectum.)

Unhappy in their marriages, two of the royal daughters-in-law, Margaret and Blanche, found alternative entertainment. Described as "feisty and shapely," twenty-year-old Margaret was the ringleader. Across the river from the Louvre was the Hôtel de Nesle, an old palace renovated as an overflow residence for visiting royals. With eighteen-year-old Blanche, Margaret turned it into a personal playground where they could party with their lovers, the brothers Gautier and Philippe d'Aunay. The third daughter-in-law, Jeanne, more happily married, knew of their activities but kept silent, and may have even joined in. Philip's chamberlain, Enguerrand de Marigny, also knew what was going on, but the princesses made it worth his while to shut up and collaborate.

Reliable records of what took place in Tour de Nesle are scarce, but rumors abound. It's said that servants combed Paris for sexual partners, who, after a few nights of orgy, were murdered by the d'Aunay brothers and their corpses, each wrapped in a shroud weighted with a cannonball, dropped from the tower into the Seine.

The scandal broke in 1313. On a visit from England, Isabella presented her brothers and their wives with embroidered and jeweled purses of the sort that, before clothing had pockets, everyone wore hanging from their belts. (The criminal to watch for in a crowd wasn't the pickpocket but the cutpurse.) Returning later that year to Paris, Isabella saw the purses she'd given to Margaret and Blanche now being worn by the d'Aunay brothers. Furious, she told her father, who had the d'Aunays arrested. Under torture, both confessed to adultery with Blanche and Margaret. Jeanne was cleared.

The château and tower were demolished in 1665. In the seventeenth century, Cardinal Mazarin, successor to Richelieu as France's behind-the-throne plotter and foreign minister, grabbed the site for a palace to house his collections of art and jewels. Margaret, Blanche, and their murderous entertainments might have disappeared into history had not

Alexandre Dumas retold a highly colored version of the tale in his 1832 play *La Tour de Nesle*. As with his *Three Musketeers*, it brought a forgotten era vividly back to life.

To help find the original Tour de Nesle, I recruited my actor friend Pierre. Trained at the Royal Academy of Dramatic Art in London, he has what the trade calls a "good address"—the ability to wear period costumes as if they are as much his everyday clothing as T-shirt and jeans.

He's also mastered theatrical fencing, so if anyone is producing or filming *The Three Musketeers*, he's first in line at the auditions. Too short for d'Artagnan, however, and too cheerful for the moody Aramis, he generally appears as Porthos, the most vain and swaggering of the trio, or even, when times are tough, d'Artagnan's bumbling valet, Planchet.

"But wasn't the tower demolished?" he asked as we walked down rue Mazarine.

"Well, yes," I said, "but that doesn't mean there's nothing to see."

Like rue de Seine, its parallel street to the west, rue Mazarine once ended at the river. Today, the former Mazarine palace blocks the way, its high blank wall looming over the narrow thoroughfare.

The closer we came to the river, the more Pierre exercised his imagination.

"You could imagine Mazarin himself being carried

along here in his sedan chair," he said. Swirling an imaginary cloak, he reached for the hilt of a nonexistent sword and made a few sketchy passes. "You never saw my Cyrano, did you?"

"Did anyone?" I said. "How long did it run? A week?"

"Ten days. Including matinees." He gloomily sheathed his fantasy blade. "That damned nose . . ."

As with the three musketeers, there really was a Cyrano de Bergerac. Savinien de Cyrano de Bergerac was born in 1619 and died in 1655. Rejected by women and mocked by men because of a honker the size of an Idaho potato, he developed a skill with both sword and words that made him famous, and inspired Edmond Rostand to write the play that became a star vehicle for generations of actors.

When Pierre played Cyrano, he exaggerated the nose even more—an unwise decision, since sweat and stage lighting softened the gum that kept it in place. During his biggest scene, where Cyrano attacks a man who has mocked him, defeating him in a duel both of blades and repartee, Pierre's wax nose sagged, then fell off entirely.

Generally, the French don't make fun of big noses, of which there is no shortage. (A certain facial type, common in France, features a nose so prominent that people joke *"Il peut fumer sous la douche"*—"He could smoke a cigarette under the shower.") However the sight of Pierre suddenly bereft of his most important facial feature was too much for one reviewer. He gleefully recalled what British critic Kenneth Tynan said of a similar loss experienced by Orson Welles in a London stage production of *Moby Dick— Rehearsed*. Laurence Olivier called his film of *Hamlet* "the tragedy of a man who could not make up his mind." Tynan joked that Welles's performance was the tragedy of a man who could not make up his nose.

The Seine was on its best behavior as Pierre and I stepped out onto the palace's wide paved forecourt. This was where the original tower stood, conveniently close to the Seine and its capacity to swallow even the darkest secret.

Opposite, across the Pont des Arts, the Louvre sat in solitary majesty. The last king to occupy that particular palace, the gawky, clumsy young Louis XVI, was happiest when he was tinkering in the company of the court lock-smith, dreaming up intricate new gadgets like some teenager building model planes. When occasionally he came to Paris from Versailles, he stuck to the Louvre. His habit of strolling along the roof, staring down at his subjects hurrying about their business, reflected his inability to understand the hopes and needs of a nation growing ever more resentful. His ignorance would survive to the very moment he mounted the guillotine on Place de la Révolution on January 20, 1793.

Though they lived four centuries before Louis and Marie Antoinette, the pleasure-seeking and murderous residents of the Tour de Nesle fell no less disastrously. Once word got out of their orgies, King Philip had no choice but to make an example of them.

The d'Aunays were brutally executed, less for adultery than for lèse-majesté—disrespect to royalty. Blanche and Margaret, forced to watch their lovers tortured to death, had their heads shaved and were imprisoned in remote castles. Margaret was specifically condemned to a tower cell exposed to all weathers, Blanche to a dungeon underground.

Jeanne, left to enjoy the Hôtel de Nesle on her own, carried on much like her sisters-in-law. According to legend, she too took a lover, the young poet and philosopher Jean Buridan, and, once she wearied of him, tried to have him liquidated in the traditional manner.

Either her servants were clumsier or Buridan smarter, since he was still alive when her servants wrapped him in a shroud and threw him into the Seine. Forewarned, he'd summoned some of his students to lurk in a barge filled with hay. As it broke his fall, the students dumped a large rock into the water to mislead the assassins, and rowed off into the night. Later, Buridan resurfaced in Germany, where he enjoyed a long career as philosopher and theologian. His story became sufficiently famous for François Villon to write in his ballad "Ballade of the Ladies of Bygone Times": "Where is the queen who ordered that Buridan be thrown in a sack into the Seine?"

Looking around the esplanade, Pierre said, "I was always sorry I never got to play *La Tour de Nesle*. Remember that scene where Buridan takes the queen back to his cheap lodgings?"

Striking a pose, he waved an arm around an imaginary room.

"'I shall speak to you standing and not with head bowed, because here you are a woman and not a queen. Here there is only a man and a woman; and because the man is quiet and because the woman trembles, it is the man who is king.'"

"But look what happened to Buridan," I said. "He ended up in the Seine."

"Well, that's true," Pierre conceded. "But what an exit, old boy. What an exit!"

THE BANKS OF THE SEINE

The Seine at Quai de Conti, where the Tour de Nesle once stood, tells the story of Paris. The banks were swamp until stone abutments and esplanades provided moorings for the barges that brought commerce to the expanding city. Bridges spanned it, creating their own mythology. On the Pont de l'Alma, the statues of four soldiers once stood guard at the pylons' bases. Three fell to modernization. Only an African soldier, known as a Zouave, survives—his post, barely a meter above the rushing waters, making him a useful gauge of the river's height. Parisians don't say "The Seine is high" but rather "The Zouave's feet are wet."

(Zouaves feature in another piece of Parisian slang. Rumors of African males' generous sexual equipment made the contents of their baggy red uniform trousers a source of fascination to some women. Where an Englishman, to indicate extreme skepticism, might say "Pull the other leg—it's got bells on it," Frenchmen of the old school will respond to a particularly outrageous claim by saying, "Oh, sure—and my sister's hand in a Zouave's trousers.")

At the foot of rue Mazarine, the palace looms on the right, narrowing the street and submerging it in shadow. The street was submerged differently in January 1910, when winter rains flooded the sewers and Metro tunnels, forcing water into the streets. A plaque at shoulder height on the wall marks the high point of the waters.

The Paris city government is forever experimenting with new ways of paving the streets. In the 1890s, it replaced stone cobbles with blocks of wood. This minimized the clop and rattle of horse cabs and buses, just as straw was once strewn in front of a mansion where someone lay ill. That the Seine might flood never crossed anyone's mind—until 1910, when the soaked blocks swelled, turning streets into impassable jumbles of wood. After that, cobbles and asphalt became the rule.

Wooden block streets along the Seine during the flood of 1910.

9

EATING OUT

Show me another pleasure like dinner which comes every day and lasts an hour.

CHARLES-MAURICE DE TALLEYRAND

TODAY, ALMOST EVERY CAFÉ IN PARIS SERVES FOOD, BUT before the arrival of the grill oven and the microwave, the choice of places to eat was calibrated precisely. Such terms as *"café," "crèmerie," "brasserie," "bistro," "bouillon,"* and *"estaminet"* all had meanings as specific as *"pharmacie"* or *"tabac."*

If speed mattered more than price, you ate at a bistro, named for the Russians soldiers who, following Napoleon's defeat in 1815, thronged Paris, demanding food *bistri*—quickly. For a cheaper meal, one chose a *bouillon*—literally "soup." At these large restaurants, often run by the state or the church, the poor could get soup and bread. Universities underwrote similar canteens for students.

Those who preferred to drink their lunch went to an estaminet—defined in 1802 by the Académie Française as "a hangout of drinkers and smokers." The standard drink of the estaminet was beer; also the case with a brasserie—literally "brewery." Some brasseries, notably Brasserie Lipp, opposite the cafés Les Deux Magots and Flore, did brew their own beer on the premises, but others appealed to altogether different appetites. Jean Émile-Bayard calls this type of brasserie "the smoke room par excellence, a place where one imbibed a brew of detestable quality in a promiscuous gathering of dubious femininity"—not much different, in atmosphere at least, to a twentieth-century topless bar.

Before the 1860s, women serving food or drink in a restaurant were generally members of the proprietor's family. That changed when a café owner on rue de la Banque, according to Emile-Bayard, "had the idea of substituting waitresses for his sole waiter. He wrote therefore to one of his colleagues in Marseilles asking him to find him a new staff, and soon received the visit of several strapping girls who had been recommended to call upon him in Paris. The buxom waitresses from Marseilles soon became popular and the neighboring cafés were deserted." In specifying that the girls came from Marseilles, where the Corsican mafia managed prostitution, Bayard hints that these girls were available for extra employment after hours.

Crèmeries offered no such "off the menu" specialties. They sold only dairy products and cheese. Most had no tables. Rather, shelves lined the walls, loaded with some of France's hundreds of cheeses. Others were prepared fresh in the large back room, while more pungent varieties matured in the cool of the cellar.

Behind the counter, the owner and his wife and daughters would have ladled fresh milk into cans you brought with you. They also sold eggs, crème fraîche (sour cream), *fromage blanc* (cottage cheese), and *fromage frais*, a mixture of crème fraîche and slightly soured skim milk. Butter, either *doux* (unsalted) or *demi-sel*, was carved with a wire from a muslin-wrapped ten-kilo block *à la motte*, in a mound shaped by the bowl in which it arrived from the farm.

They also sold the plump, round black-topped *gateau fromage*, its moist and crumbly interior revealing it as the ancestor of modern cheesecake. Another specialty was the Fontainebleau: *fromage blanc* mixed with whipped cream was piled into a small bowl and topped with a square of muslin to prevent it smearing your other purchases. Once home, you sprinkled it with sugar, the crunch and sweetness of which contrasted deliciously with the slightly sour cream.

Crèmeries dwindled around 1900. Iceboxes, the precursor of the refrigerator, allowed housewives to stock up on dairy goods rather than buy them fresh each day. Students too, particularly those from the country, wanted the egg-and-cheese dishes they enjoyed at home. Once *crèmeries* installed tables and began to serve *omelets au fromage*, the transition to restaurant was only a matter of time.

CRÈMERIE RESTAURANT POLIDOR,
41 RUE MONSIEUR LE PRINCE

In Woody Allen's *Midnight in Paris*, Hollywood screenwriter Gil Pender is swept back to the Paris of the 1920s, where he meets all his heroes and heroines, among them Ernest Hemingway, who lectures him on writing during a rendezvous at Crèmerie Polidor.

One sees why Woody chose the Polidor. As much museum as restaurant, it has barely changed since it opened in 1854. The uneven tiled floor, the mirrors interspersed with advertisements in Belle Epoque lettering, the communal tables with red-and-white-checked gingham cloths, even the notorious "Turkish" toilet, little more than a ceramic-rimmed hole in the floor, all recall a more robust era of cheap eating and rowdy discussion. Among the oddest survivals is a bank of lockboxes at the back of the main room where regulars leave their napkins each day until they accumulate enough stains to need laundering.

The Polidor menu has barely changed in a century. This is country cooking, robust and unsubtle:

sausage, pâté, slow-cooked beef and pork accompanied by mashed potatoes, cabbage, and lentils. If you're hoping for fillets of sea bass with balsamic vinegar reduction, seek elsewhere. That said, the *pintade*—guinea fowl—braised with cabbage is a dish at which even the great Escoffier would not have turned up his nose.

Crèmerie Polidor.

❊ · 10 · ❊

UNDERGROUND

*One shouldn't look for existentialists at the Café de
Flore. They're all holed up in the cellar clubs. After the
caves of the Vatican come those of St-Germain-des-Prés.
That's where the existentialists, waiting no doubt for the
atomic bomb, which to them is so dear, will from now on
drink, dance, love.*

ANONYMOUS, "HERE'S HOW THE TROGLODYTES
LIVE IN ST-GERMAIN-DES-PRÉS,"
SAMEDI-SOIR, 1949

B<small>Y SURRENDERING TO</small> G<small>ERMANY IN</small> 1940, F<small>RANCE</small>
averted war but paid a high price for peace. Via the puppet
collaborationist government headquartered in Vichy, the
Nazis bled the nation of food and fuel, plundered its art,
slaughtered its citizens, deported young men as forced labor
and Jews to death in the gas chambers of Ravensbrück and
Auschwitz.

Rationing of electricity dimmed the city of light. Evoking the disease so long endemic in Saint-Germain, author Arthur Koestler wrote, "Paris is melting away as if infected with consumption."

The city survived only by chance. As the Reich expired, Hitler ordered it reduced to rubble. Explosives were packed into its great buildings, but at the last minute the military governor, General Dietrich von Choltitz, ignored Hitler's orders and surrendered the capital intact to de Gaulle's Free French.

There was damage enough, however. Four years of neglect left Paris weatherworn and crumbling, and the residents starved into lethargy. The communists, made optimistic by their leading role in the resistance, expected to sweep into government but failed dismally. Once their power was broken, de Gaulle mocked the idea of a one-party France. "How can a single idea govern a nation that has two hundred and forty-six different kinds of cheese?"

For the postwar generation, the wind blew not from the Soviet Union but the United States. Now GIs, not Nazis, crowded the cafés. Waitresses and whores learned English as they had picked up German, barmen mixed martinis, and cooks made hamburgers. Everyone chewed gum. Lucky Strikes and Camels became the new currency.

"America symbolized so many things," wrote Simone

de Beauvoir in 1949. "It had stimulated our youth. It had also been a great myth—an untouchable myth." She could speak with authority, having just returned from the United States and an affair with novelist Nelson Algren, author of *The Man with the Golden Arm* and *A Walk on the Wild Side*.

Her memories of prewar Paris made the city all the more drab. With most hotels closed for lack of heat, linen, food, or staff, she reluctantly took a room in the Hôtel d'Aubusson on rue Dauphine, in the heart of Saint-Germain. "The hotel was a filthy shack," she wrote, "with an icy stone staircase that smelt of mold and other unnamable odors. My room was a shambles; an iron bedstead, a wardrobe, a table, two wooden chairs; peeling walls and a miserable yellow light from a single bulb. The kitchen doubled as a toilet."

Even so, Saint-Germain was jumping. As four years of accumulated Hollywood movies flooded French cinemas, scores of new weeklies and newspapers erupted onto the newsstands, satisfying a long-stifled hunger for photographs, information, and opinion unmuzzled by censorship.

Kids danced what they called "bebop"—actually jive or jitterbugging. True bebop, an intricate and often dissonant style of jazz only then emerging in New York, would not reach Europe for years. Prewar bohemians were surprised, visiting the cellar clubs of postwar Saint-Germain, to hear the same New Orleans jazz to which they'd danced thirty years ago, but played now by the likes of trumpeter-novelist Boris Vian.

Everyone was watching American crime films and reading pulp detective stories. To kick off his own publishing house, Éditions du Scorpion, Vian even wrote a pastiche American thriller, *J'irai Cracher sur vos Tombes* (*I Will Spit on Your Graves*). Supposedly his translation of a book by "Vernon Sullivan," an African-American whose work was banned in his own country, it featured a black hero pale enough to "pass" for white, an advantage he exploited to indulge in interracial sex and finally murder. His cover blown, Vian was convicted of obscenity and fined 100,000 francs, but recouped his losses by selling the film rights, only to be repelled by the movie's inauthenticity. At the premiere screening in 1959, he shouted, "These guys are supposed to be Americans? My ass!" and collapsed with a fatal heart attack.

Like the Beats of Greenwich Village a few years later, Paris's new bohemia came with a uniform and a way of life. What poet Thom Gunn wrote of Elvis Presley—"He turns revolt into a style"—went double for Saint-Germain. Unable to buy the T-shirts, jeans, leather jackets, and sneakers worn by their American counterparts, would-be hipsters dressed in the least French-looking clothing they could find: checked lumberjack shirts, black cotton trousers, and tennis shoes.

Apartment living was scorned. De Beauvoir, Sartre, and Albert Camus all later moved to the Hôtel La Louisiane. Perched above a busy food market at the intersection of rue de Buci and rue de Seine, it had long been a cheap flop for intellectuals. Before the war, British writer and editor Cyril Connolly had lived there with his mistress and their pet ferrets, which they fed on raw horse liver.

In an ambiance somewhere between student residence and theatrical boardinghouse, guests were free to experiment, ignored by a management indifferent to who shared whose bed. But the bohemian disdain for bourgeois comforts was mostly a pose. Many so-called existentialists were weekend rebels only, slipping back to parental homes in more fashionable *quartiers* where they could enjoy a bath and home-cooked meals. Jean-Paul Sartre shared a spacious apartment with his mother, overlooking the square in front of Saint-Germain church. The iconoclastic Vian had a degree in engineering, and kept a home in Montmartre where brass plates on the door proudly advertised both his avocation, "Writer," and his profession, "Engineer." One room was a workshop, containing his neatly arranged collection of tools.

Saint-Germain's queen was Juliette Gréco. Arriving from the south at the end of the war, she became the darling of the cafés. Dark-haired and voluptuous, often barefoot and invariably dressed in black, she used her husky voice, high cheekbones, and liquid brown eyes to hypnotic effect. Installed at La Louisiane, she was photographed sharing a bed with her best girlfriend—and also lover? Nobody knew, but the question piqued the interest of everyone from trumpeter Miles Davis, with whom she had an affair, to Jean Cocteau, who gave her a small role in *Orphée*.

De Beauvoir had less reason to favor the new bohemians of Saint-Germain. The Hôtel d'Aubusson shared its basement with the most fashionable nightclub in Paris, and therefore its noisiest. It was called Le Tabou and its emblem was Gréco.

Juliette Gréco.

LE TABOU,
33 RUE DAUPHINE

A simple café until 1946, Le Tabou blossomed once it received official permission to stay open twenty-four hours a day, a concession to the bike messengers employed by publishing house Hachette, on nearby rue Christine. Working unsocial hours, they had nowhere else to meet and eat in a city where most cafés closed by two a.m.

Night birds soon drifted there as other bars closed. To accommodate them, the club split in two. While the ground floor remained a bar, open to all, the cave, once used for storage, became a dance club where Boris Vian led the band.

Not everyone could enter. To push aside the curtain and descend the narrow stone stairs required a nod from Juliette Gréco.

Initially a fan of Gréco, writing that she had "millions of poems in her voice," Sartre became increasingly irritated by her cult. In 1951, he posted a notice in Saint-Germain's most fashionable bookshop, Le Divan.

Be advised that existentialism, the philosophy, has nothing whatsoever to do with the existentialism at large in St. Germain-des-Prés. When Juliette Gréco opened the Café Tabou, she was asked who she was. The answer was "an existentialist." The press seized on the word. That band of check-shirted youngsters who haunt St. Germain-des-Prés came to be known as existentialists. They bear no relation to me, nor do I to them.

Residents of rue Dauphine were no more welcoming of Le Tabou's clientele. Noisy patrons spilling out at dawn risked having chamber pots emptied over their heads. It's unlikely the victims noticed. So much cigarette smoke collected in the unventilated cellar that, according to Vian, it resembled a tunnel through which a locomotive has just passed, while sweat so saturated the air that a loaf of bread left on a table through the course of an evening deliquesced to "the state of moldy porridge."

Le Tabou lingered for a few years before other cafés became more chic. The cellar reverted to its original function as a storeroom, and it wasn't until 2015 that the hotel acknowledged its historical importance with a plaque in the lobby.

Juliette Gréco survived longer than Le Tabou. During the 1950s, as one of Hollywood mogul Darryl F. Zanuck's many European mistresses, she appeared in a few mediocre films.

She had more success as a singer in such clubs as La Rose Rouge on rue de la Harpe in the Latin Quarter, the deficiencies of her voice balanced by her beauty and some sultry material. (One of her biggest hits was "Deshabillez-Moi"—"Undress Me.") Seeing her perform in 1950, journalist Kaye Webb wrote:

> *"Le petit oiseau noir chante a minuit" ["The little black bird sings at midnight"] said a Paris paper writing of Juliette Gréco, whose clothes, fringe and unconventional behavior (which includes walking the boulevards in bare feet, and sitting on the kerb to rest) are faithfully copied by girls all over the quarter. She opened the program on the hour, appearing dramatically between the red velvet curtains wearing a black dress, with long black hair and unsmiling black eyes. She sang poems by Sartre and Jacques Prévert in an odd deep voice, infinitely stirring to those under twenty-five and touchingly immature to those over thirty.*

As Gréco's fame declined, that of Sartre spread with a rapidity all the more amazing for the fact that almost nobody knew his work and fewer understood it. Asked to define "existentialism," he claimed a journalist made up the term, which he rejected as meaningless.

Outside France, he was known simply as a French intellectual with a devoted following of young bohemians. In the 1957 movie *Funny Face*, Audrey Hepburn manages a Greenwich Village bookshop but dreams of visiting Paris to meet Emile Flostre, inventor of empathicalism, a vague creed that her costar, Fred Astaire, summarizes as a streamlined version of "Do unto others . . ." Rather than explain Sartre's appeal as a thinker, the film makes Flostre a suave fraud who preys on his prettier acolytes—not so different from Sartre after all.

Gréco and de Beauvoir could have been among those who paused one morning in 1947 to watch photographer Robert Doisneau taking pictures in the street outside Le Tabou. Unlike some photographers who stalked their subjects, intent on capturing what one of them, Henri Cartier-Bresson, called "the decisive moment," Doisneau staged his images, directing his subjects until the pictures told the story he wanted. "I don't photograph life as it is," he said, "but life as I would like it to be."

That morning, he was shooting three young men and

two girls crammed into an ancient automobile. The pale shadowless light, their expressionless faces and mussed hair, and the presence of Le Tabou's facade in the background tell us they have just emerged, ears ringing, minds numbed, after a night of jiving, booze, and disputation, and are focused only on coffee, bed, sex.

Key to the image is the automobile, a 1926 Renault 6CV NN. Known as the "People's Car," it was France's equivalent of the Model T Ford. As the petrol ration dwindled to four gallons a month, a few of these underpowered antiques reemerged from sheds and barns, to be cleaned up by young enthusiasts and defiantly put back on the road.

To further thumb his nose at the culture of austerity, the owner of this car, poster artist and theatrical designer Yves Corbassière, painted its bodywork in eight-inch squares of yellow and black. As it became fashionable to autograph the yellow squares, it gathered numerous celebrity signatures, among them Errol Flynn's.

Corbassière's car and Doisneau's images capture something of the postwar generation: its hectic gaiety in the face of the nation's fiscal and moral bankruptcy, a search for new reasons to enjoy life in the wake of war. Pressed to explain his reasons, Corbassière would simply have shrugged. Doisneau knew what he wished to achieve, but for Corbassière the act was its own justification: the true existential response.

Yves Corbassière and his decorated car outside the Tabou, 1947.

11

THE CUP THAT CHEERS

Some folks put much reliance
On politics and science;
There's only one hero for me!
Its praise we should be roaring,
The man who thought of pouring
The first boiling water onto tea!

A. P. HERBERT

In my Australian childhood, a single solution served for every conceivable disaster. House burned to the ground in a bushfire? Dingo stolen your child? Wife decamped with your best friend? Never mind. Have a nice cup of tea.

In extreme cases, tea was augmented with an over-the-counter tranquilizer. Bex, the brand leader, advertised itself with the slogan "Stressful Day? What you need is a cup of tea, a Bex and a good lie down."

A spoonful of fine white powder folded into a square of paper, prescient of the future packaging of cocaine, Bex dissolved instantly in any hot liquid. And while its mixture of aspirin, phenacetin, and caffeine did calm you, it was universally acknowledged that what did most good was the tea, fortified with two or three heaping spoons of sugar and, in extreme cases, a generous gloop from a can of sweetened condensed milk.

Since my generation grew up on tea, it was, naturally, among the first things we rejected. No cup of Earl Grey or Lapsang souchong, be it ever so lovingly brewed, could compete with the cliché cappuccino, however bitter the brew and greasy the froth.

In my case, that enthusiasm survived until I arrived in France. In a culture so reliant on the café, the quality of coffee would, I assumed, be of paramount importance. I could not have been more wrong. What matters to the French is the *idea* of coffee, the pretext it offers for a conversation tête-à-tête, the rituals of sugaring and stirring, which, like the fidgeting that accompanies the lighting of a cigarette, become with repetition a manual choreography, a gestural dance.

As to how the coffee tastes . . . well, visitors from such coffee-sophisticated cultures as Italy and the Netherlands have been known to gag on a French *express*. My most

Taking tea, Paris, 1921.

coffee-savvy friend, an American poet who divides her
time between Paris and Naples, will accept an invitation to
coffee *chez moi* only if permitted to bring a paper sack of her
preferred Neapolitan grind. Not trusting even Paris water,
she also insists on brewing it only with Evian.

Given the social significance of coffee in France, it's understandable that tea took a back seat. This was ironic, since when the two beverages arrived from the east, they were equally popular. Tea even had the edge because of its appeal to women, who disliked the harsh unsweetened coffee of the time. Tea was the beverage of the salon, a delicate infusion that, surprisingly, was often sipped from the saucer.

Though it's no shame to order tea in a Paris café, don't expect anything more than a small metal pot of more or less boiling water and a paper-wrapped tea bag. Serious tea drinkers brew their own at home, buying in bulk from one of the two primary suppliers, Kusmi, an old firm of Russian origin, or Mariage Frères.

MARIAGE FRÈRES,
13 RUE DES GRANDS AUGUSTINS

The Mariage brothers, Nicolas and Pierre—pronounced, incidentally, as three syllables, *Mar-EE-arge*—were among the merchants sent out by Louis XIV in search of new and exotic products. In particular, he urged them to find sources for tea, which both the king and his adviser Cardinal Mazarin drank to alleviate gout.

Nicolas Mariage traveled to Persia and made deals for spices with the Mughal Empire, while Pierre set up trading links with Madagascar. The tradition was carried on by their sons, culminating in the founding in 1845 of Auguste Mariage et Compagnie, importers of tea from China and Ceylon.

Although today Mariage Frères sell their teas all over the world, there is no location more agreeable to sampling them than one of their Paris tea shops, preferably the branch tucked away on this quiet Saint-Germain street. Its wooden frontage and oak interior, the shelves lined with antique metal containers, create a tranquil setting in which to explore its five hundred blends.

Fashion has carried tea a long way from the mahogany-colored fluid of my Australian childhood. Experts, in fact, insist that "there is no such thing as 'tea'" and prefer to speak of infusions or tisanes. Herbs, flowers, spices, even cannabis, may, either mixed with conventional tea or brewed in their own right, contribute to the sipping experience. The "tea" in which Marcel Proust famously soaked a few crumbs of a madeleine, inspiring the thirteen volumes of *À la Recherche du Temps Perdu*, wasn't tea at all but an infusion of flowers from the lime tree, and had more to do with helping the digestion of his *tante* Leonie than any pleasure in drinking. (Caution is advised, however, in experimenting with the more exotic medicinal mixtures, some of which, as one critic unkindly wrote, "tasted like the inside of an actress's handbag.")

Occasionally, at a corner table in one of the Mariage Frères salons, one may glimpse a woman seated alone, working her way determinedly through cup after cup of almost colorless fluid. It was American author Diane Johnson who, in her charming novel *Le Divorce*, alerted me to the motives of such lone drinkers. Inevitably, this being France, they did so out of love.

Certain infusions, she revealed, offer an erotic experience that even the *Kama Sutra* fails to mention—a technique that the empress Joséphine might have exercised for the pleasure of Napoleon, famously responsive to feminine odors. One of Diane's characters explains, "If you drink a little tisane of orange and rosewater or mint, it perfumed your juices. . . . Quite a lot of tisane, though—a whole teapotful is required." To imbibe half a liter of tea simply to smell and taste good for your partner! Can there be any more touching—and French—assurance of love?

Teas, confitures, *and teapots on sale at Mariage Frères, Paris.*

12

THE KISS

Look into my eyes. Kiss me, and you will see how important I am.
SYLVIA PLATH

No CITY IN THE WORLD IS MORE ENAMORED OF THE KISS than Paris. From Auguste Rodin's lovers of *Le Baiser*, frozen in their white marble embrace, to *Le Baiser de l'Hôtel de Ville*, Robert Doisneau's photograph of a smack snatched in a crowded street outside the town hall, kisses are so promiscuously and publicly conferred that the entire city often seems bent on bestowing the Big Wet One. Even a footballer who has just netted a goal opens his arms to his team's collective embrace. Anglo-Saxon sportsmen who used to think this the limit of Gallic insanity now imitate them. How long before the custom appears in even in more sedentary leisure pursuits? Billiards? Chess?

But if the French, particularly Parisians, kiss without

restraint, it's for a reason. Like those other rituals—the nod to a neighbor, the eye contact with the concierge, the "Bonjour, m'sieur" with which one greets even the bus driver and street sweeper—kisses lubricate the abrasion inevitable in a city where more than two million people occupy a space that, just about anywhere else, would accommodate only half that number. In the hive that is Paris, the bees, rather than stinging one another, create honey instead.

As in nature, females set the standard. On first meeting a woman, it's customary to shake hands, but on parting, if the meeting has not been drop-dead disastrous, she will offer her cheek. Between females, two kisses are standard, a third indicates genuine pleasure, while enduring affection demands a fourth and even, exceptionally, a touch on the lips.

Among men, the kiss is reserved for close friends or relatives—"kissing cousins"—but also, paradoxically, for formal ceremonies: weddings, funerals, the conferring of honors. In such cases, "sealed with a kiss" means what it says. As official as a rubber stamp, the kiss confirms legality. Nobody watching Charles de Gaulle hinging his mantis-like frame to plant two smackers on the cheeks of a whiskered *poilu* just presented with a Croix de Guerre could possibly imagine he meant anything more by it than comradely respect.

After formal kisses, however, come the sexual kind. The term "French kissing" first appeared in English around 1923 to describe a kiss that employed both lips and tongue—something at which the French, traditionally, were adept. As a comic put it at the time, "The French they are a funny race / They talk with their hands and fuck with their face." (Incidentally, it's not only in English that meanings change. Time has also transformed "*baiser*," once the word for "kiss," into a synonym for "fuck." Today's polite form is "*embrasse*.")

As with most human activities, effectiveness in kissing is measured less by the "what" and the "where" than the "whom." Certain Paris locations do, however, by repute, possess a sexual significance beyond the ordinary.

To slightly amend Andrew Marvell, "The grave's a fine and private place / And some, I think, do there embrace." Cemeteries are popular sites for a discreet meeting of lip and lip. Favorites include the shared resting place of Simone de Beauvoir and Jean-Paul Sartre in Montparnasse Cemetery, and that of Gertrude Stein and Alice Toklas in Père Lachaise. Gay couples bond by the tomb of Oscar Wilde in the same cemetery, which also contains a monument to Abelard and Héloïse. This is less popular as a kissing location since it's doubtful the great lovers are actually buried there. Also, as Héloïse's uncle had Abelard castrated, their tomb can evoke negative thoughts of one's potential in-laws. When New York literary critic and wit Alexander Woollcott paid a visit, he left as his tribute not a bunch of roses but a pair of walnuts.

Equally dubious are the Square d'Orléans, where George Sand first met pianist Frédéric Chopin, a troubled relationship at best, and the bench near no. 6 Place des Vosges, opposite the former home of sexually voracious novelist Victor Hugo. Notoriously, Hugo entertained a succession of mistresses who arrived and left by a side door of which the bench gives a good view—hardly an encouragement to constancy.

Leda and the Swan. Relief by Achille Valois.

THE FONTAINE DE LÉDA,
JARDIN DU LUXEMBOURG

Many who kiss prefer the open air, and an audience. Why be in love and hide it? What is the kiss if not a show, with its own decor and dialogue, its performances, even—sometimes humiliatingly—its reviews?

For outdoor romance in Paris, one can hardly improve on the Jardin du Luxembourg. Generations of lovers have necked on its green-painted metal chairs, scuffed hand in hand through the fallen chestnut leaves, or nuzzled surreptitiously at the Fontaine de Médicis, with its overarching plane trees and statue of Polyphemus, one-eyed giant of Ovid's *Metamorphoses*, surprising his mistress Galatea in the arms of her lover Acis.

But couples seeking something more erotic will slip around behind this baroque reconstruction (c. 1866) to the earlier, less lavish, and often disregarded Fontaine de Léda, which backs onto it. This originally stood in the middle of what is now rue de Médicis. Rather than demolish it, the architects bonded it to the Fontaine de Médicis, where, half hidden among the trees, it became a sly encouragement to disgraceful behavior.

From a shaded pool, a single waterspout bubbles before a relief by Achille Valois illustrating how Zeus assumed the form of a swan to ravish the beautiful Leda. The graphically drooping neck of the satiated bird, the figure of Cupid, shrinking, almost aghast, from what has just transpired, and a languid Leda exhibiting what William Blake called "the lineaments of gratified desire" so shocked critic Amaury Duval in 1812 that he announced "the ideas it calls to the imagination [make it] hardly a suitable subject for a monument placed before the eyes of the public."

But hiding it only attracted more admirers. Writing in 1926, Sisley Huddleston, the *Times of London*'s man in Paris, noted the popularity of this part of the gardens. "The alley from the Odéon Theatre to the Place Medicis constitutes the principal promenade of the younger generation of students, who go backwards and forwards with measured steps, engaged in animated conversation for hours." Today, it's lovers who, indifferent to the runners panting by on the jogging track, take advantage of the trees that shade the pool. The presence of onlookers may even intensify the experience. Only those kissing know for sure, and they aren't talking.

13

CLOSED HOUSES, OPEN MINDS

*The "ladies" see no harm in your coming, merely to
inspect them. They will parade before you in frankest
nudity, and dance with one another in a mirror-walled
room, so that of their charms you may miss nothing.*

BRUCE REYNOLDS,

PARIS WITH THE LID LIFTED, 1927

THOUGH BROTHELS HAVE EXISTED IN ALL COUNTRIES AND
eras, France conferred on them a degree of respectabil-
ity. Known as *maisons closes* or *maisons de tolérance*, they
enjoyed quasi-legal status, part of the same liberalization
that decriminalized homosexuality. A brothel could op-
erate openly, providing it registered with the police and
the women submitted to monthly medical examinations.
Pimping remained illegal and "living off immoral earn-
ings" a crime, but men could own a brothel, provided

a woman, the traditional madam, managed it on their behalf.

Investment in a brothel was no more disreputable than financing restaurants or shops; less so, in fact, since Napoleon scorned commerce, which was best left to the English, that "nation of shopkeepers." Shops smelled of cheese and disinfectant, the *bordel* of perfume and champagne.

Novelist Marcel Proust owned an interest in two homosexual brothels, and the syndicate behind Paris's most prestigious establishment, Le Chabanais, included members of the rigidly conservative Jockey Club—the same club, paradoxically, that banished the Vicomte Charles de Noailles, one of its most distinguished members, when he financed the anticlerical Surrealist film *L'Age d'Or* of Luis Buñuel and Salvador Dalí.

No stigma was attached to owning a brothel or spending an evening there. *Le Guide Rose*, a regularly updated booklet, listed the best establishments, even recommending particular women for their beauty or expertise. As Maupassant explained in *La Maison Tellier*, a brothel was a business like any other.

> *Madame Tellier, who came of a respectable family of peasant proprietors in the department of the Eure, had taken up her profession just as she would*

have become a milliner or dressmaker. The prejudice which is so violent and deeply rooted in large towns does not exist in the country places in Normandy. The peasant says, "It is a paying business," and he sends his daughter to keep an establishment of this character just as he would send her to keep a girls' school.

Businessmen used brothels as a kind of club, socializing with the women without necessarily having sex. The geisha houses of Japan and "key clubs" of Western cities in the 1960s offered the same relaxed and slightly disreputable atmosphere that encouraged plain speaking. Describing Madame Tellier's house, Maupassant, a sexual athlete and no stranger to *bordels*, sketched some typical clients.

They went there every evening about eleven o'clock, just as they would go to the club. Six or eight of them; always the same set, not fast men, but respectable tradesmen, and young men in government or some other employ, and they would drink their Chartreuse, and laugh with the girls, or else talk seriously with Madame Tellier, whom everybody respected, and then they would go home at twelve o'clock! The younger men would sometimes stay later.

This collusion between the bourgeoisie and the demi-monde ended abruptly in 1946, when brothels were made illegal in France, part of the moral backlash following the end of the war. The closure affected not only the capital's 180 registered houses but also 1400 others nationwide. In theory, their premises were to be allocated to newlywed veterans hoping to start families. In practice, most young couples declined to begin married life in a one-time whorehouse, so the buildings either reverted to their original function or became conventional apartment houses.

In common with most morally motivated social engineering, the closure of France's brothels made a bad situation worse. The pimps returned, along with those sexually transmitted diseases that monthly medical examinations had kept in check. Forced back to the streets, prostitutes now serviced their clients in *hôtels de passe* that rented rooms by the hour.

To men for whom the brothel had been a vital amenity, the change was catastrophic. Among the most deprived were those who did not dare be seen entering a *hôtel de passe*. They included policemen and military officers in uniform but, even more potentially disastrous for their profession, priests.

That four brothels once flourished in the shadow of the

Salon at the Rue des Moulins *by Toulouse Lautrec.*

huge church of Saint-Sulpice merely underlines their ambiguous role in French society.

No. 7 rue Saint-Sulpice housed a brothel called the

Le Choix 1 *(Gustave Assire)*

Abbey, while on the second floor of no. 15, in a former hammam, or steam bath, a lady calling herself Alys operated a small business with a couple of girls. At no. 26, Chez Christiane catered, according to *Le Guide Rose*, to *"sodomie et sado-masochisme"*—services similar to those on offer at the largest of the four, Miss Betty's at no. 36.

Only a regular client of these establishments would know of their existence. The use of a red light to identify a brothel, first used in the United States around the end of the nineteenth century, never caught on in France, where discretion was preferred. Some houses adopted deceptively domestic names. The man who said he spent the evening at My Uncle's or at My Sister's Place gave no hint of what he was really doing.

Houses such as Chez Christiane used the names of their proprietors. Others were identified by their addresses. The most exclusive, Le Chabanais, sometimes called the House of All Nations because of its rooms decorated in Japanese, Persian, and Turkish styles, took its name from the short street in the second *arrondissement* on which the building stood. A reference to *"le 122"* could only mean 122 rue de Provence, just as "Rue des Moulins" signified one of the brothels where Henri de Toulouse-Lautrec spent weeks at a time, drinking and sketching its women.

The style of architecture could also advertise its use. Metropolitan brothel owners often chose tall, narrow buildings, with one or two rooms on each floor, and a single entrance. By placing an angled mirror on each landing, the madam could look over the staircase from her parlor on the top floor and check which doors were closed, and whether any staff were not earning their keep.

MISS BETTY'S BROTHEL,
36 RUE SAINT-SULPICE

No. 36 rue Saint-Sulpice is tall and narrow. Unlike the buildings on either side, which show the house number in blue on a white enameled metal plate, the colorful ceramic plaque above its door is large, almost ornate.

In other respects, however, Miss Betty's establishment was exceptional since it catered almost exclusively to priests.

The reason was practical. Until the 1930s, shops selling plaster statues and religious vestments and regalia filled the streets around the church of Saint-Sulpice. A country *curé*, unable to patronize a brothel in his hometown, might, while in Paris for the day to pick up some new vestments, feel safe in paying a call on Miss Betty. Afterwards, he could even cross the street to the church, confess his sin, perform his penance, and still catch the last train home. Making it even more discreet, a back entrance from the lobby opened onto innocently busy rue Guisarde, a street lined with restaurants.

Both the Abbey and Miss Betty's offered ecclesiastical specialties. Miss Betty's facilities included "a torture chamber, with a cross of St. Andrew [i.e., shaped like the letter X—a crucifix would have been too sacrilegious]; diverse pincers, hooks and chains; a gibbet for those who found that a noose around the neck provoked an erection. The torture chamber called Satan's Hell gave a foretaste of damnation; the client was tormented by she-devils who offered no respite."

In the Sacristy, named for the room where priests donned their robes, secular clients could try on priestly vestments, or watch girls model them while otherwise naked. Elsewhere, a confessional waited, its carpet and wallpaper crimson rather than the traditional brown. Within, the usual roles could be reversed. How much more exciting to confess one's sins, or have those of others confessed to you, when priest or penitent wore the other's clothes, or, even more piquantly, nothing at all.

THE SHOW MUST GO ON

Life's but a walking shadow, a poor player
That struts and frets his hour upon the stage
And then is heard no more. It is a tale
Told by an idiot, full of sound and fury,
Signifying nothing.

WILLIAM SHAKESPEARE, *MACBETH*

RUE DE L'ODÉON, AT THE SOUTHERN MARGIN OF SAINT-Germain, has a significance out of all proportion to its size. A street of one block, built in 1760, sloping up from boulevard Saint-Germain to the colonnaded facade of the Théâtre de l'Odéon, it was the first in Paris to have a side-walk. Before then, only a fifth of the city's streets were paved. The prosperous traveled on horseback or by car-riage, not setting foot on the ground until they entered the paved courtyard of the house they were visiting. The poor were left to slog through mud in winter and choke on dust in summer—an incentive to stay close to the cobbled lanes that make up a large part of Saint-Germain and the Quartier Latin.

Rue de l'Odéon and the streets on either side once formed part of the Paris pleasure grounds of the Princes de Condé, who stayed there when visiting the capital from their château at Chantilly. Never lucky with money, the Condés were forced to sell the property in the mid-1700s. All that survives are names. The street east of rue de l'Odéon is rue de Condé. That to the west bears the honorific accorded to the Condés as relatives of the king. Since the Prince de Condé was traditionally addressed as "Monsieur le Prince" (Mr. Prince), the street on the other side of rue de l'Odéon is rue Monsieur le Prince.

The playwright Beaumarchais, author of *The Marriage of Figaro*, lived on rue de Condé, while numerous literary figures lodged on rue Monsieur le Prince, convenient to the nearby Sorbonne. The crème de la crème, however, gathered on rue de l'Odéon. It is no coincidence that Sylvia Beach chose it to set up her English-language bookshop Shakespeare and Company, eventually to publish James Joyce's *Ulysses*, or that Thomas Paine wrote the *Rights of Man* on the same street, and Robert McAlmon published *Three Stories and Ten Poems* by the then-unknown Ernest Hemingway. The aromas of resentment, nostalgia, and am-

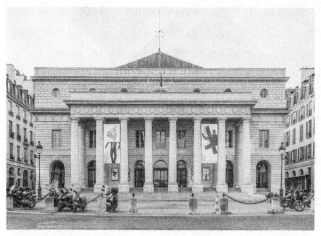

The Odéon Theatre today.

bition that permeate this street can't be ignored. It is the perfume of Saint-Germain.

The Théâtre de l'Odéon has stood at the head of rue de l'Odéon since 1779, a symbol of privilege, undisturbed by revolution, unshaken by war, and the survivor of two fires, each of which left it a burned-out shell. To those living in the cramped rooming houses of Saint-Germain, it appeared as a sentinel, barring the pious Quartier Latin from the shameless bohemia of Montparnasse.

In 1959, André Malraux, de Gaulle's minister of culture, assigned direction of the Théâtre de l'Odéon, then a poor relation of the national theatre, the Comédie-Française, to Jean-Louis Barrault and his wife, Madeleine Renaud. French theatre had few bigger stars. In addition to his innovative stage productions, Barrault had acted in such movies as *La Ronde* and, in particular, *Les Enfants du Paradis*, a recreation of nineteenth-century Paris theatre life in which he starred as the mime Dubureau.

For the Odéon, Barrault mounted an adventurous program, ranging from classics by Racine and Shakespeare to Eugène Ionesco's absurdist *Rhinoceros*, Jean Genet's provocative *The Screens*, and the first production of Samuel Beckett's *Happy Days*, a personal triumph for Renaud.

Given its size and location, the theatre was an obvious target for the students of the nearby Sorbonne when they rebelled in May 1968. Storming inside, they demanded that Barrault allow them to hold a meeting there. Swept up in the general euphoria, he not only agreed but also made a speech in support of their revolt.

It was a signal for chaos. Black and red flags flew over the facade as ten thousand people surged through the building, ripping up the upholstery and the curtains, breaking into the costume store, stealing what could be worn and defecating on the rest. Students strolled the streets of Saint-Germain in gowns designed for performances of Molière and Beaumarchais.

A "Committee of Occupation" urged "the systematic

sabotage of the cultural industry, especially the industry of show business, in order to make room for true collective creation. Never again must a ticket be sold in the ex-theatre of France. The only theatre is guerrilla theatre!"

In vain, Barrault tried to reason with the student leaders, Jean-Jacques Lebel and Daniel Cohn-Bendit, a.k.a. Danny the Red. What exactly was "guerrilla theatre"? Who would perform it, and where? What of actors and technicians? How were they to earn a living? If the Odéon was an "ex-theatre," then those who worked in it must be "ex-people."

"But here is a living creature named Barrault in front of you!" he challenged. "What are you going to do?"

Nobody had an answer.

As France ground to a halt in a general strike, President de Gaulle abruptly left the country, destination unknown. This convinced the new alliance of students, factory workers, and the Communist Party that he had thrown in the towel, and that a promised election would end his administration. In fact he had flown to Baden-Baden in Germany, where General Jacques Massu, commander of the French forces on the Rhine, assured him the army would cooperate if he declared martial law.

Nothing so extreme was necessary. In the June election, the silent majority reelected de Gaulle. Ordinary people just wanted a return to normality—the daily papers, radio, and TV—even if the government controlled their content. And it was, after all, almost August—holiday time. As the weather became warmer and the beach more enticing, the issues so inflammatory in May seemed far away. No longer spoken of as a rebellion, the disturbances were demoted to "*les événements*"—events.

When the police and army ignored appeals to evict the occupiers, Barrault realized Malraux had thrown his theatre to the students "like a bone to a dog." A shrewd move, it discouraged them from attacking more prestigious locations such as the headquarters of ORTF, the national broadcaster, or the Académie Française, housed in the former palace of Cardinal Mazarin.

As Barrault, in the wake of the occupation, surveyed the ruin of the Odéon, Malraux delivered the coup de grâce and dismissed him, on the pretext that, in making a welcoming speech, he had sided with the students.

Abandoned by both sides, Barrault turned to volunteers for assistance and looked to other venues. In a former ice rink, mostly used for wrestling matches, he presented *Rabelais,* a play mingling the life and work of Francois Rabelais, and employing inflatables to create the monsters of his *La Vie de Gargantua et de Pantagruel.* After that, he pitched a tent inside the disused Gare d'Orsay railway station and staged innovative adaptations of Nietzsche, Voltaire, and Kafka. The "ex-actor" and his "ex-theatre" outlasted not only *les événements* of 1968 but also Malraux's tenure as minister and even de Gaulle himself, whom Barrault survived by twenty-four years. As for the Théâtre de l'Odéon, it has outlived both.

Rue de l'Odéon viewed from our building.

THE ODÉON FORECOURT, CAFÉ VOLTAIRE, AND LA MÉDITERRANÉE

Following the last major renovation of the Odéon theatre in 2013, an outdoor café was opened on its forecourt. Operating only in the summer months, it's a pleasant reminder of the semicircle of cafés that once faced the theatre. From the 1880s, Café Voltaire was a favorite. At its tables, Henry Murger collected the stories that Puccini would set to music in *La Bohème*. (The original Café Momus, where most of the second act of the opera is set, was actually on the Right Bank, on rue des Prêtres Saint-Germain l'Auxerrois, squeezed between Pont Neuf and the Louvre, but elements of the Voltaire survive in his description.)

The offices of publishers now occupy most of the former café premises, with the partial exception of La Méditerranée. A restaurant rather than a café, it features front windows looking out on the view enjoyed by Gauguin and Verlaine. Jean Cocteau, dining there in 1960, was asked by the management to sign the *livre d'or*, or guest book. As flamboyant as ever, he responded with a drawing—his vision of the Mediterranean, on the shores of which he then lived. Over a yacht-dotted sea under a blazing sun, he superimposed the profile of his sexual ideal: a husky hunk with the profile of Orpheus, though in this case with the eye replaced by a spiny fish that gastronomes recognized as the *rascasse*, an essential ingredient of the classic seafood stew bouillabaisse.

Shrewdly, the restaurant reproduced his drawing on its china and linen. It harmonizes with the decor: murals by Christian Bérard and Marcel Vertès, lithographs by Picasso and, of course, Cocteau, not to mention a photo gallery of former patrons: Orson Welles, Charlie Chaplin, and a cluster of crowned heads.

Jean Cocteau's design for the Méditerranée restaurant.

15

THE LAST BOHEMIAN

To tend young goats on Attic hills
And weave with Raymond Duncan,
I'm sure would aggravate my ills
And make me fey and drunken.

E. B. WHITE, 1935

IN THE FIRST HALF OF THE TWENTIETH CENTURY, MANY foreigners came to France in search of the freedom to behave in a way their own countries viewed as disreputable, if not illegal. Prominent among them were San Franciscans Isadora Duncan and her brother Raymond. Isadora pioneered modern dance, while Raymond pursued a more eclectic career as poet, sculptor, publisher, designer, actor, and philosopher.

As children, both Duncans were fascinated by ancient Greece. At six, Isadora was teaching other children a form of dance based on movements from Greek sculpture.

In 1898, their mother took them to Europe. Paris became Isadora's spiritual home. Among her idols was the sculptor Auguste Rodin. Heavily bearded, dressed in a monk-like robe, he was every inch the great artist. "He gazed at me with lowered lids, his eyes blazing," she said, "and then, with the same expression that he had before his works, he came towards me. He ran his hands over my neck, breast, stroked my arms and ran his hands over my hips, my bare legs and feet. He began to knead my whole body as if it were clay."

Having memorized her dimensions, Rodin was anxious to explore further, but Isadora, to her later regret, fended him off. She soon made up for it, taking numerous lovers of both sexes, including Paris Singer, heir to the sewing machine fortune, who supported her until her death in 1927.

Touring Europe with her troupe, the Isadorables, Duncan became so synonymous with extravagant behavior, both on stage and off, that the poet Dorothy Parker nicknamed her "Duncan Disorderly." Isadora died on the French Riviera, expiring as she had lived: flat broke, a little drunk, and speeding towards sexual gratification. Seated next to a new lover in his racing car, she didn't notice the fringe of her shawl becoming entangled in the rear wheel. Dragged from her seat onto the road, she died instantly.

While Isadora danced, her brother gravitated to

Greece. He and his Greek wife, Penelope, bought a villa near Athens that they decorated in the ancient style. He adopted the same style of dress, and insisted his family and any visitors do the same. Author John Glassco called him "a walking absurdity who dressed in an ancient hand-woven Greek costume and wore his hair in long braids reaching to his waist, adding, on ceremonial occasions, a fillet of bay leaves."

Following Isadora to Paris, Raymond started a commune on the edge of the Bois de Boulogne, where he aimed to re-create life in Attic Greece. Liberal France was a willing audience for his theories. Unwed mothers, rejected by their families, brought their children to the commune, where they were raised by the community. During World War I, Duncan visited convalescent hospitals and taught weaving to wounded soldiers. He also showed housewives how to spin knitting yarn from the raw wool with which most mattresses were stuffed.

In 1919, he bought a building at 31 rue de Seine, in the heart of Saint-Germain. Above the columned entrance, the words "Akademia Raymond Duncan" identified what he modestly called "the Artistic Centre of Paris." As well as teaching weaving and fabric printing, Duncan expounded his "Philosophy of Action" and sold sandals, togas, and scarves made at the commune. The Akademia also had a theatre, but without seats. In authentic Greek fashion, the audience reclined on couches.

Duncan estimated ten thousand women attended his dance classes, including James Joyce's daughter Lucia. A number of them shared his bed, among them American writer Kay Boyle whose part-time job as secretary to Gladys Palmer, heiress to a large British baked goods manufacturer, led to one of the odder literary encounters of the time.

Having become a princess by marrying Bertram Brooke, "White Rajah" of the Malay state of Sarawak, Palmer felt deserving of a memoir, and asked Boyle to ghostwrite it. A tea party was held to introduce the princess to Paris literary society. Boyle invited Gertrude Stein and Alice Toklas, but Raymond Duncan also turned up, uninvited: "looking," wrote literary historian Humphrey Carpenter, "like a Roman emperor and speaking like a mid-Western farmer."

Stein, to everyone's surprise, greeted him as an old friend. Their families had known one another in California, and the two grew up together, though had scarcely met since. A bantering conversation followed about childhood baseball games and Duncan's adolescent experiments with alcohol. Before long, Stein's sturdy feet were shod in Duncan sandals.

When Penelope Duncan died in 1925, Raymond mar-

ried one of his students, who was offended by his illegit-
imate children among those at the commune, the living
evidence of his busy love life. Abruptly announcing that
he now found pregnant women "disgusting," Raymond
ceased offering sanctuary to unwed mothers, and began to
skimp on food, shoes, and clothing for the children already
there, even forcing them to sleep in a barn on the pretext
that they needed more fresh air. The next time Duncan
spoke in public, angry mothers stormed the stage, shouting, "We came to you in the hopes of finding beauty and
goodness. We found only bad faith, deceit, violence, and
hypocrisy." The commune closed shortly after.

During the 1930s, Raymond toured the United States,
lecturing and presenting his versions of Greek dramas.
Journalists resented his habit of giving interviews while reclining on a couch, from which, wrote one, he "discoursed
about the lack of art among us provincials."

His audiences included a group of African-American
art lovers, rated by *The New Yorker* as "one of the haughti-
est and most cultured of the Harlem intellectual claques."
During his talk, Duncan described how, on a visit to the
Riviera, he'd enjoyed the music of a Harlem jazz group,
Charlie Johnson's Paradise Band.

"And so," he said, "I wanted to come back and meet
you all, the brothers and sisters of Charlie Johnson."

Frosty silence greeted this information. Johnson's group was formerly the house band at Smalls Paradise, a basement speakeasy whose waiters performed the Charleston on roller skates while balancing trays of bootleg booze. None found the comparison flattering.

Refusing to leave Paris during World War II, Duncan was among the first at the American embassy to welcome the Allies in 1944. Although almost eighty, he hoisted the Stars and Stripes over the building and "sang *Yankee Doodle Dandy* until he was hoarse."

In a postwar Paris dominated by America and existentialism, the ethics and aesthetics of ancient Greece became increasingly anachronistic. "Duncan followers are mainly aging maiden ladies," wrote a reporter in 1949. "They foregather at the Akademia every Saturday afternoon when the Master presents the 'Stars of Paris,' usually young artists or writers who read their own work or play the piano with concentrated fervor. The Master writes poetry himself and recites it at every opportunity."

Duncan died aged ninety-one in 1966, the last of Saint-Germain's bohemians. His declining years offered one more moment in the limelight. In 1955, Orson Welles produced a documentary series for British TV called *Around the World with Orson Welles*. An episode devoted to Saint-Germain-des-Prés included a visit to the Akademia.

As the camera enters a darkened workshop where men chip desultorily at slabs of stone, Welles's distinctive voice booms through the gloom, and a figure in toga and sandals shuffles from the shadows.

"Ah, good mawnin'," says Duncan jovially—sounding less like a sage of old Athens than a Kansas corn farmer.

As Welles thanks him for agreeing to be filmed, Duncan looks a little rueful.

"Unfortunately I'm not a *beau garçon*," he says. "I've been much used by life. Perhaps your cameras will not be so successful. The public like round, baby-like faces."

Was this a gibe at Welles's chubby features? If so, Orson chose to ignore it. Rather, as he followed Duncan around the Akademia, hearing how he wove his robes on his own loom and hand-made books on his own printing press in a typeface he designed himself, he may have felt a twinge of recognition and regret. Throughout his career, Welles strove for a similar control over his own work, and always failed. Perhaps such autonomy could never be achieved except at the price Duncan paid: to become an eccentric, a recluse, and, to many, a laughingstock.

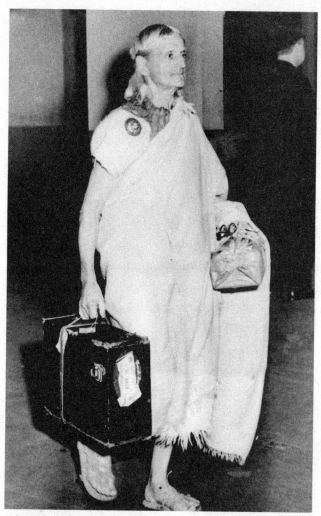

Raymond Duncan, 1948.

RAYMOND DUNCAN'S AKADEMIA,
31 RUE DE SEINE

"Have you ever heard of Raymond Duncan?" I asked my French wife, Marie-Dominique.

Since she was raised in Saint-Germain, she might conceivably have seen him. In toga and sandals, he must have been hard to miss.

She put down her book and thought for a moment.

"Wasn't there a shop?" she said at last.

Now that I raked my memory, I also vaguely remembered a murky window plastered with posters, and inside, showcases of . . . something or other. Might the Akademia still have existed when I made my first visit?

No. 31 rue de Seine was only a ten-minute walk away, but of the Akademia there was no sign. The colonnaded facade had disappeared, as had the bold lettering above it. Shops flanked the big double doors of the porte cochere, but neither offered goatskin sandals for sale. However, above the door a small plaque announced:

GEORGE SAND (1804–1876) HABITA A CETTE MAISON EN 1831 PUIS RAYMOND DUNCAN Y CREA L'ACADE-MIE DE 1929 A 1966.

Sand and Duncan in the same building? It made a kind of sense. If the paths of a cross-dressing novelist and a toga-wearing sage were ever to converge, it would be in Saint-Germain.

The door to no. 31 had a standard electronic entry system. Pushing the single button below the number pad, I heard the latch click. A wide paved passage led through the building to a sunlit courtyard, barred by a heavy metal grille. Evidently the building had reverted to its original use as apartments. But even though the courtyard was now open to the sky, I recognized the space where Welles had filmed. Apparently Duncan had roofed it over to create a workshop.

Propped against the courtyard wall on either side were four of the rough stone reliefs seen being carved in the Welles film. In one of them, a man plucked at a lyre, watched quizzically by a goat. In others, potters spun clay on a wheel, worked at benches, or used sledgehammers to split stone. The workmanship was crude, even unfinished. What were they meant for? What did the present owners of these apartments make of them?

But there was nobody to ask. I could have rung the bell at the concierge's loge, but she probably knew nothing. Like Raymond Duncan, the Akademia, and his commune, these slabs belonged to a past as remote as the ancient Greece that had inspired them. I left them to their sunny obscurity.

Reliefs carved by Raymond Duncan, 31 rue de Seine.

16

SLEEPING WITH THE ENEMY

*Our spirit of enjoyment was stronger than our spirit of
sacrifice. We wanted to have more than we wanted to
give. We tried to spare effort, and met disaster.*

HENRI-PHILIPPE PÉTAIN

DURING THE NAZI OCCUPATION OF FRANCE BETWEEN 1940
and 1944, both of the shadowy armies competing for the
shaky will of a defeated nation looked to the arts for recruits.

Germany's long-term plans called for France to become
the Reich's source of food and cheap labor, but also a prime
tourist destination. While its farmlands supplied meat,
grain, and fruit for the new Europe, Paris and the Côte
d'Azur would be maintained as resorts.

Rather than crush France's flourishing show business,
the occupiers adapted it. Certain cinemas were designated
Soldatenkino—cinemas for troops, showing German films—
and some cafés admitted only men in German uniform.

Pressed to offer entertainment to the occupiers, café owners, rather than disturb their regular clientele, compromised by transforming their *caves*, or cellars, into *boîtes de nuit*—nightclubs. Since space was limited, jazzmen provided the music—a complication, since Hitler had declared jazz "decadent." In addition, the best players were Jewish, gypsy, or black, all proscribed under Nazi racial laws.

Fortunately the Luftwaffe *Oberleutnant* in charge of entertaining the troops, Dietrich Schulz-Köhn, was a jazz fan. Even before the war, he'd been a friend of such French experts as Charles Delaunay of the Hot Club of France.

Given wide latitude by his superiors, Schulz-Köhn designated Jewish musicians as "*Wirtschaftlich wertvolle Jüden*," economically valuable Jews. Gypsies and players of African or West Indian extraction received equivalent documentation, exempting them from deportation. To convince the musicians of his good intentions, Schulz-Köhn was photographed in uniform with a racially mixed group of jazzmen in front of La Cigale, one of the city's oldest music venues. Grateful musicians nicknamed him "Doctor Jazz." Django Reinhardt, France's leading jazz performer and a gypsy, was on tour in England when the Germans invaded, and could have sat out the war there. Instead he returned to Paris and played publicly throughout the occupation.

Django Reinhardt.

Most writers kept their heads down and had as little contact as possible with the Germans. Others found it politic to make a show of cooperation, particularly if they wished to continue being published.

In October 1941, eight prominent French authors attended a literary conference in Weimar at the invitation of Nazi propaganda minister Joseph Goebbels. One of them, Marcel Jouhandeau, justified his presence by announcing grandiloquently, "I would like to make my body a fraternal bridge between Germany and us."

Others went because it was good business, and benefited accordingly. Among them, Pierre Drieu La Rochelle became editor of the important literary monthly *Nouvelle Revue Française* and Robert Brasillach of the pro-Nazi magazine *Je Suis Partout* (*I Am Everywhere*).

Among the expatriates, some became active collaborators. They included Irish patriots who believed Germany's promise that Ireland would be given independence from Great Britain under the Third Reich. Even before the war, poet and editor Ezra Pound had moved to Italy and become a vociferous supporter of Mussolini. Sisley Huddleston, veteran correspondent for the *Times of London*, so admired Marshal Pétain that he became a French citizen and pledged himself to Vichy—a rash decision that led to his imprisonment in 1944 by the Free French.

Another British turncoat, William Joyce, became the radio voice of the Reich, broadcasting propaganda in an affected upper-class English accent that earned him the nickname "Lord Haw Haw." The humorist P. G. Wodehouse, creator of the imperturbable valet Jeeves, was living in France when the Germans invaded. Captured in 1940, he broadcast a number of light comic pieces for radio from occupied Paris that incensed the British authorities. Wodehouse never returned to Britain, spending the rest of his life in the United States, while Pound was first imprisoned, then deemed insane. William Joyce, convicted of high treason, was hanged.

Having accepted the reality of occupation, many French celebrities chose to make the best of it. Couturier Coco Chanel shared a suite at the Ritz hotel with her German lover, and used Vichy's anti-Semitic laws in a bid to claw back control of her perfume business, which she'd sold to a Jewish firm. Actresses Mireille Balin and Arletty lived openly with Germans, Arletty excusing her behavior with a famous quip: "My heart is French, but my ass is international." Jailed after the war, she had to be brought in handcuffs to the studio where director Marcel Carné was recording the dialogue for her most famous film, *Les Enfants du Paradis*.

Among painters, Picasso and Matisse remained in Paris, but kept low profiles. Singer Tino Rossi, Charles Trenet, and club owner Suzy Solidor all performed for Nazi audiences and broadcast on German-controlled Radio-Paris. "We understood that terrible things were happening in Poland and Austria," Maurice Chevalier said, "but Parisians don't really care about anything but Paris. I guess we feel we are doing our share by giving laughter and gaiety to the nation." Rashly, he staged a photo opportunity during which he drained a bottle of Vichy water, a gesture he found difficult to live down. Cartoonists mocked his earlier patriotic hits such as the 1939 "Tout Ça, Ça Fait d'Excellents Français" ("That's How Good Frenchmen Are Made"), which celebrated the fact that, no matter what their politics or the state of their health, all Frenchmen rallied to the defense of their country.

Anglophile writer and collaborator Bernard Faÿ intervened to save Gertrude Stein and Alice B. Toklas, relocating them in the remote village of Culoz under the protection of the local *commissaire de police*. In gratitude, Stein translated a selection of Marshal Pétain's speeches and suggested to her American editor Bennett Cerf that he publish them. Fortunately for her reputation, he squashed the idea. Unlike many literary and artistic collaborators who were jailed for periods ranging from a few days to some months, then quietly released, Bernard Faÿ remained in prison until 1951, when Alice Toklas funded his escape to Switzerland.

The only prominent writer executed for collaboration was Robert Brasillach, shot by firing squad. Though he was unapologetically anti-Semitic, his hasty trial and execution aroused suspicion. Was de Gaulle avenging the death of his friend Georges Mandel, in which Brasillach may have played a part? Brasillach's last words were *"Vive la France quand même!"* ("Long live France anyway").

Brasillach's homosexuality could have been a factor in his condemnation, and some French gays were imprisoned and murdered, but many others had "a good war," none more so than Jean Cocteau. "Openly and comfortably gay," wrote one historian, "Cocteau moved in all the best circles. His need for attention and his easy morals got him rides in the limousines of many wealthy Parisians and occupiers who found him amusing."

Among litterateurs, opposition was patchy; writers make poor partisans, and while many professed support for the resistance, few offered concrete help. Sartre, after nine months as a prisoner of war, spent the rest of the occupation writing. Albert Camus, more active, edited the antioccupation magazine *Combat*. Éditions de Minuit (Midnight Editions) published clandestine booklets of patriotic verse, so small they could be dropped down a drain if the owner was searched. Pseudonyms disguised the work of Louis Aragon and Paul Éluard.

Some writers, including André Breton and Antoine de Saint-Exupéry, fled to New York, where "Saint-Ex" refused to speak anything but French as long as France was occupied. Another who remained in Paris vowed not to speak a word in any language until the invaders were ousted, and not even to *look* at a German.

When Samuel Beckett was on the run from the Gestapo, Sylvia Beach hid him and his girlfriend in the apartment above Shakespeare and Company. In 1940, she closed the shop after enraging a German officer by refusing to sell her only copy of James Joyce's *Finnegans Wake*. Her companion, Adrienne Monnier, also closed her Maison des Amis des Livres.

At the end of 1942, Beach was among the 350 women, most of them Americans, rounded up and shipped to the spa town of Vittel. For six months, they lived six to a room in the former Grand Hotel, once fashionable but now rundown, unheated, and surrounded by barbed wire. After her release, Sylvia was too ill to reopen Shakespeare and Company. Adrienne, prey to delusions and driven nearly insane by the ear affliction tinnitus, killed herself in 1955. Sylvia returned to America, but came back to France to live in the little apartment above the then-closed shop. She died there in 1962, alone and largely friendless. Her body wasn't discovered for some days.

Café reserved for German military personnel, Paris, 1943.

Some French institutions aroused particular enmity from the Germans, among them the Café d'Harcourt on boulevard Saint-Michel. A literary meeting place since the nineteenth century, it attracted Irish writers in particular, notably James Joyce, John Millington Synge, and Oscar Wilde. In November 1940, students staged a protest there on the anniversary of the armistice that ended World War I. In revenge, the Germans closed it down and turned the premises into a bookshop, the Librairie Rive-Gauche, selling only works approved by the Nazis. The shop, under armed guard, remained open throughout the occupation, patronized almost exclusively by Germans. Students periodically smashed its windows and defaced the facade. On one notable occasion, a lone resistant blew it up by packing a hollowed-out volume with dynamite. The book was Karl Marx's *Das Kapital*.

Although postwar films and fiction represented the resistance as a well-organized clandestine army, anti-German resistance consisted of numerous groups, each with its own agenda and often hostile towards one another. Best organized were the Communists, who emerged from the war as a powerful political force.

Many more were criminals who'd escaped from prison in the confusion of the invasion and joined the *maquis*, named for the undergrowth in which partisans hid between raids. In David Dodge's novel *To Catch a Thief*, filmed by Alfred Hitchcock, jewel thief John Robie is a former *maquisard* who, with the rest of his gang, is rewarded with parole after the war. The story was founded in fact. Many Corsican resistants went on to lucrative postwar careers in the drug business. One of them, Jean Jehan, masterminded the heroin smuggling operation dramatized in the film *The French Connection*.

Hotel Lutetia.

Famous for enjoying their comfort, the Germans seized Paris's most luxurious locations as their headquarters. The Luftwaffe took over the Luxembourg Palace, digging up its formal gardens and planting vegetables. Dietrich von Choltitz, military governor of the city, grabbed the eighteenth-century Hôtel Meurice, while the Abwehr counterintelligence service of Admiral Wilhelm Canaris commandeered the Hôtel Lutetia.

HÔTEL LUTETIA,
CORNER OF BOULEVARD RASPAIL AND RUE DE SÈVRES

In choosing the Lutetia, the Abwehr reflected the forward thinking of the Third Reich. The Meurice, Crillon, Bristol, and other top hotels dated back centuries, but the Lutetia—named for the Roman name for Paris—was built in 1910. Art nouveau stone vines and grapes spill from its balconies, a reminder that this land had previously been under vineyards. Its art deco interior, however, has more in common with the first-class lounges of transatlantic liners.

As imposing as such a liner, the hotel looms over a wide intersection, within sight of the world's first department store, Bon Marché. The placement was no accident. Louis-Charles Boileau and Henri Tauzin designed it with the store in mind. Guests were expected to shop at leisure, have their purchases delivered to their rooms, and show them off in the hotel's lounges and restaurants.

But modern hotels bored wealthy tourists, particularly Americans, who favored the venerable Meurice, Crillon, and George V. Fortunately, European celebrities liked its international style, while the subtle lighting and lofty ceilings of the cocktail lounge flattered its more theatrical clients. Charles de Gaulle spent his wedding night there in 1921. Art collector and gallerist Peggy Guggenheim checked in regularly, as did revue and movie star Josephine Baker. Even James Joyce, not averse to luxury despite his assumed air of Irish frugality, wrote part of *Ulysses* in one of its suites.

Under the occupation, the Lutetia also sheltered collaborators targeted by the resistance. Otto Abetz, the Nazi ambassador to Vichy France, used it to entertain foreign businessmen eager to share the plunder of France. It was less hospitable to those fugitives from Nazism who paused there too long while planning an escape to Britain or the Americas. Trapped by the swift German advance, many were sent to internment camps, then deported to Germany. Others met their fate at the hands of the Gestapo in the more secluded sixteenth *arrondissement*.

In August 1944, General de Gaulle pointedly ordered the Lutetia transformed into a repatriation center for survivors of the concentration camps. Pale and emaciated, dressed now in rags, they shuffled through the lobby where they were once welcomed as guests. Relatives scanned notice boards for news of loved ones. Juliette Gréco paced the sidewalk outside the hotel for days before being reunited with her mother and sister. A plaque on the wall facing boulevard Raspail commemorates the hotel's role in the liberation of Paris, but not its discreditable part in the occupation.

17

$1000 A YEAR

Paris is noisy, jostling, crowded and cheap.
ERNEST HEMINGWAY, 1921

IN DECEMBER 1921, ERNEST HEMINGWAY AND HIS WIFE Hadley arrived in Paris and headed straight for Saint-Germain. Their hotel, the Jacob et d'Angleterre, at 44 rue Jacob, came recommended by Sherwood Anderson for both its centrality and economy.

Early in the new year, in a high-spirited article for the *Toronto Star Weekly*, Hemingway assured readers that "a Canadian with $1000 a year can live very comfortably and enjoyably in Paris." He went on: "Our room costs twelve francs a day for two. It is clean, light, well-heated, has hot and cold running water and a bathroom on the same floor. That makes a cost for rent of thirty dollars a month."

Other advantages of life in Saint-Germain included inexpensive travel on the Metro and good meals at modest prices in the nearby Pré aux Clercs restaurant. "The dollar, either Canadian or American, is the key to Paris," he concluded. "With the U.S. dollar worth twelve and a half francs and the Canadian dollar quoted at something over eleven francs, it is a very effective key."

F. Scott Fitzgerald shared his wonder at what could be bought for a buck. In "Babylon Revisited," his poignant story of a reformed drunk returning to Paris in hopes of repairing his life, his character recalls with faint surprise that "he had never eaten at a really cheap restaurant in Paris. Five-course dinner, four francs fifty; eighteen cents—wine included."

Though, in representing Paris life as carefree, romantic, and cheap, Hemingway was telling readers what they wanted to hear, reality proved less exhilarating. Once they got over the novelty of subsisting on what amounted to pocket change, they realized Hadley's $5000-a-year trust fund, while covering essentials, didn't run to full-time hotel-and-restaurant living, particularly if it also had to fund trips to Switzerland to learn to ski, Spain for the running of the bulls at Pamplona, the Côte d'Azur for holidays where they mingled with the celebrity houseguests of wealthy dilettantes Gerald and Sara Murphy.

By the time the article appeared, they had rented a fourth-floor apartment at 74 rue du Cardinal Lemoine on the sleazier edge of Montparnasse, a district of cheap bars, ugly whores, and the rough crowd that worked in the rue Mouffetard street market. Life for such people was, in Thomas Hobbes's phrase, "solitary, poor, nasty, brutish, and short"—or, in Hadley's words, their neighbors were "the salt of the earth—but some dirt had got into the salt."

By local standards, the Hemingways were prosperous. Ernest could afford to rent a study in a nearby house, and they even had a maid, Marie. She worked for five hours each morning and also prepared their evening meal, to be heated up after she left. To clean the floor, she shuffled doggedly through the rooms with rags tied to her feet. In later life, both legs would be amputated—in part, speculated Hadley, because of the hours spent in such grinding labor.

A public dance hall occupied the building's ground floor, its accordion music filtering up the stairs and through the open windows. The Hemingways sometimes spent an evening there. Like most expatriates, they viewed such places as "local colour," unaware of their importance in a culture that strictly monitored relations between the sexes. In the neutrality of the *bal musette*, single men and women could meet with the minimum of formality. Etiquette required that dancers remain silent on the floor, not even exchanging names. On the tightness with which you clutched your partner, however, there was no restriction.

The French fiancée of Spanish film director Luis Buñuel taught him the *java* and *le fox* so that they could embrace in the *bal musette* with an intensity forbidden everywhere else. Since, in this speechless environment, an inability to speak French was no handicap, Hadley was much in demand as a partner, while Ernest, in her words, "grabbed anything he could get."

Hadley's trust fund proved increasingly inadequate, and after the birth of their son, the lure of the annual $50,000 enjoyed by both Pauline Pfeiffer and her sister, Virginia, proved too tempting for Ernest. Following a brief involvement with Virginia, terminated when he discovered her bisexuality, he took up with the willing and enthusiastically heterosexual Pauline, whom he later married.

Dancers in a bal musette.

ERNEST HEMINGWAY APARTMENT,
6 RUE FÉROU

While Hemingway was motoring around Italy in 1927, Pauline, helped by Ada MacLeish, wife of poet Archibald MacLeish, chose the top-floor apartment at 6 rue Férou as their new home. In addition to a large bedroom, a sitting room, and a dining room, it contained two smaller rooms suitable for use as a study or for a maid. (Though Ernest and Hadley argued over who would retain the invaluable Marie, the room finally became a nursery.) A generous kitchen and bathroom, plus two flush toilets, completed the amenities—luxurious by comparison with the apartment in Montparnasse Ernest occupied with Hadley.

With the franc pegged at twenty-five to the dollar, the apartment's annual 9000-franc rental amounted only to the same thirty dollars a month Ernest and Hadley had paid at the Hotel Jacob. However, when legal fees, plus an under-the-counter payment of "key money" to the outgoing tenant, pushed up the price, Pauline, rather than dip into her trust fund, appealed to her uncle Gus, wealthy proprietor of Hudnut, a perfumes and hair-products company.

Gustav Pfeiffer paid for the apartment and supported the couple for years, buying their cars as well as the Key West house that became their principal home, and funding the $25,000 safari that inspired *Green Hills of Africa*. Hemingway rather stiffly dedicated *A Farewell to Arms* to his benefactor, the US edition simply "To G.A. Pfeiffer" and the British printing, even more tersely, "To G.A.P."

The normally ebullient Ernest was ill at ease amid the antique Spanish decor chosen by Pauline for rue Férou. On the first visit of his old friend Morley Callaghan, he spontaneously challenged Callaghan to an improvised boxing match, during which they sparred around the apartment, trying to avoid damaging the furniture.

On another occasion, a skylight fell on his head, leaving a lifelong scar. Hemingway embellished this story over the years. In some versions, the accident took place in another's house when he was sober. In others, it was at rue Férou when he was drunk. The most elaborate retelling blamed "a bohemian named Jerry Kelley [who] went to use the can before departing. Instead of pulling the chain for the toilet, he grabbed hold of the skylight cord, gave it a heavy yank, and down came the skylight in a shower of glass [which] gashed my head open."

Archibald MacLeish took Hemingway to the American Hospital, where he was stitched up by a young doctor whom Hemingway claimed was Carl Weiss, later the murderer of Louisiana governor Huey Long. (There's no evidence of this, nor does MacLeish remember the man.) Hemingway paraded his bandaged brow around Paris for weeks. Later he was evasive about his scar, not discouraging people from assuming it was inflicted in battle. As a critic wrote of him, employing an appropriate metaphor from the *corrida*, Hemingway worked very close to the bull.

Sylvia Beach admires Hemingway's injury.

☀ · 18 · ☀

BON APPÉTIT

Marie Harel, eighteenth century farmwife of the town of Camembert, has been glorified as inventor of that cheese (from which her husband cleared his fortune). Madame Harel's monument, a stone shaft, unfortunately resembles a slice of Gruyère. There is no justice.

GENÊT (JANET FLANNER), 1927

WHILE WE KNOW MUCH ABOUT WHAT THE EXPATRIATE community drank, there's surprisingly little information on what they ate. Anecdotes about food generally focus on the differences between the French and American diets. At one of Isadora Duncan's soirées, attended by a number of painters, including Moïse Kisling, waiters handed round ostentatiously expensive canapés of ham garnished with smoked oysters in foie gras. With a shudder, Kisling led a mass exodus of the French guests. "I'll treat you to white wine, a pig's head and some sardines in the first *bistro* we come to," he promised, evoking a menu that would have nauseated the Anglo guests.

Until the 1970s, French cafés served no food except croissants, and the dishes offered in restaurants were often alien to foreign visitors. Not only did the French relish horse meat and snails, their sausages resembled nothing eaten in America. Nor did they toast bread, fry bacon, or grill hamburgers. Restaurants that attracted Americans did so by recalling a lesson from World War I, and serving an unvarying menu of fried eggs and *frites*.

That they drank wine with their food was the most widely known culinary fact about the French. Journalist Waverley Root, fresh off the boat from Prohibition America, ordered a bottle of Bordeaux with his first meal. The waiter brought it without comment. It wasn't his business to explain that even the French didn't take wine with breakfast.

Used to American cafés, which served cocktails and beer, provided bar snacks or even a free lunch, and often featured some sort of musical show, as well as the opportunity to dance, tourists complained that most Paris cafés offered neither food nor entertainment, and sold only coffee, liqueurs, and brandy. They were particularly disgusted, on ordering beer, to be given Byrrh, a sweet red wine infused with quinine.

Within a few years, the larger cafés installed *bars amer-*

icaines, serving the cocktails Americans expected, but until then, visitors made do with aperitifs and digestifs. Sweet, sticky, and highly alcoholic, these made you almost instantly drunk, but also even more speedily sick. At expatriate parties, guests often mixed the dregs of three or four glasses in a grisly potion, only to vomit it explosively over the balcony into the street, indifferent to pedestrians below.

Of all expatriates, only Gertrude Stein's companion, Alice Toklas, displayed a talent for the kitchen. There's proof of her gift in both *The Alice B. Toklas Cookbook* and the girth of her partner, Gertrude Stein. That food was central to their relationship is reflected in their pet names for one another, including "Lobster" and "Cake."

Many expatriates dined at the Stein-Toklas table, but few shared Alice's enthusiasm for cooking. At their Saturday evening soirées, she led the females into the kitchen so that Gertrude could have the men to herself. This irritated such women as Sylvia Beach and Djuna Barnes, who had no interest in exchanging recipes or discussing Alice's new electric mixer.

The list of contributors to Toklas's famous cookbook, published in 1954, when she was in her seventies, confirms their indifference. Battling a failing memory, she asked former guests to supply their favorite recipes or remind her of dishes eaten at her table. Most who did were European, predominantly French, and almost none were artists. One exception, poet and painter Brion Gysin, who briefly owned a restaurant in Tangier, sent, tongue in cheek, a recipe for Haschich Fudge ("good for warding off the common cold in damp winter weather"), which Toklas, probably not getting the joke, included in the book.

Although Hazard, Montparnasse's largest grocery store, proudly displayed an "English Spoken" sign over its front door, no expatriate mentions shopping there, or anywhere else. It was cheaper to employ a housekeeper—even Toklas and Stein had one—who doubled as a cook. Usually women from the country, they had learned in the family kitchen to make basic stews and soups, and soon became familiar with American tastes.

Hemingway might praise Brasserie Lipp's *cervelas* sausage, served on cold boiled potatoes dressed with olive oil, but he and Hadley seldom ate out. When they lived on rue du Cardinal Lemoine, they ate dinner prepared by their maid, Marie. In between, Ernest snacked on fruit, and chestnuts roasted on his workroom fire. Taking a daily walk after spending the morning writing at the Closerie des Lilas, he would cut through the Jardin du Luxembourg to avoid restaurants with their tempting aromas, then drop in on Gertrude and Alice to eat with them, or sample one of the liqueurs made by macerating fruit in brandy.

Since few rooming houses had kitchens, single Frenchmen and -women ate where they worked. Many cafés began as coal and wood yards that offered a hot drink to chilled and weary deliverymen. Street vendors sold coffee, hot milk, bread, soup, roast potatoes, and stew. Around noon on weekdays, pop-up restaurants appeared in the city center. Firing up stoves in otherwise empty stores, women prepared a few basic dishes that one could eat there or take away. Writing in 1899, Georges Montorgueil described one such woman.

> *There she kept her eye on her pot au feu [beef and vegetables in broth] while peeling the potatoes that sizzled in boiling fat—the same fat that served to deep-fry a sole, or cheese puffs and donuts. A sign proposed "Soup and Beef To Go." For two sous, you got a bowl of hot beef broth; for four more, you could choose between stewed beef, mussels, boiled potatoes—and always, naturally, the classic frites.*

If you preferred cold cuts, *triperies* offered cooked tongue and tripe. Charcuteries sold ham and sausage, all of which could be eaten on the run, as could bread still warm from the *boulanger*. You still see young men and women nibbling the end of a baguette as they check their iPhones while walking back to the office, and a *sandwich jambon fromage*—ham and Gruyère cheese on a baguette—remains the most popular lunchtime snack.

Busiest of all food suppliers, however, were *fromageries*, since no product provides the synthesis of culinary and cultural satisfaction so effectively as a slab of cheese.

"Pop-up" lunchtime restaurant, Paris, 1890s.

CHEESE: A FABLE

Night comes on quickly in the mountainous forests of the Auvergne. Urging his horse along the barely visible track, the young doctor knows there's no chance of reaching town by dark.

Thoughts of wolves and even worse predators so fill his mind that he hardly believes the whiff of smoke that tickles his nostrils. Then he sees it: a tiny mill, barely visible below, where the valley narrows and the creek runs deep enough to turn the wheel.

Slipping from his saddle, he leads the horse down the steep slope, shouting until someone comes to the door. A woman—well, a girl, really. And pretty, with a soft mouth, and challenging eyes that send a trickle down his spine like cold water.

"Is your father here?"

"No—but her husband is." He fills the door behind her, fat, old, and suspicious.

In his best bedside manner, the doctor explains: the wife of the duke's son in labor . . . difficult delivery . . . misjudged the time. If they could manage a bite to eat, some straw in the barn . . .

"We turn away no traveler in these hard times,"

growls the farmer, "if you don't mind sharing our dinner, and our bed."

The meal is a surprise, not in its ingredients—bread, cheese, red wine—but in their quality. Particularly the cheese.

"Your own?" he asks the farmer, cutting another slice.

"Marie-Claude's family." He downs his second large glass of rough red. "They keep sheep in the next valley."

Lowering her eyelashes, Marie-Claude pushes the board toward him. "Help yourself."

It's not only cheese that's being offered.

When the doctor returns from watering his horse, the farmer and his wife are both in bed, the old man snoring thunderously. The girl lies next to him, coverlet turned down invitingly at her side.

"A brass band wouldn't wake him now," she murmurs. "And you heard what he said. We deny a traveler nothing."

"Nothing? Really?"

He needs no urging. Turning from the bed, he finds the cheese on the shelf where she left it. Taking it to the table, he cuts a generous slice.

The preceding story of the doctor, the lady, and his midnight snack is ancient—as old, perhaps, as the *Heptameron* of Marguerite de Navarre (1492–1549). The lesson, however, remains the same: no lust is quite so powerful as the French appetite for cheese. When, in 1947, a film, *Les Sept Péchés Capitaux* (*The Seven Deadly Sins*), retold it as an illustration of Greed, the screenwriter slightly changed the role of the wife. When she whispers, "I know what you want. Go on. Do it!" we know from her smile that she understands it's the cheese and not her body he desires. As he heads back to the cupboard, she rolls on her side with a smile and cuddles up contentedly to her oblivious husband.

When British advertising agencies introduced the ploughman's lunch into pubs in the 1960s, they flattered themselves it was their own invention. A plate of bread and cheese with a dollop of vinegary chutney on the side, it kept drinkers at the bar rather than going out to a restaurant.

Culinary historians knew the French had anticipated them by a millennium. For centuries, cheese, eaten with bread and wine, had been the midday meal for a sizeable percentage of Paris. Not only did this combination of protein and carbohydrates provide energy for a day of hard labor, the choice of a cheese from your home district could affirm one's cultural identity. The more perceptive expatriates embraced this national enthusiasm. In 1927, Janet

Flanner wrote of "goatherds, including our favorite Baptiste, whose flock parades the Quartier St. Germain at high noon." As he passed, she bought a patty of his soft homemade chèvre cheese, "at two [francs] fifty the cake, a remarkable luncheon dainty."

Cheese seller with the author, rue de Seine, 2015.

MARKET *FROMAGERS,*
RUE DE SEINE STREET MARKET

Bread, wine, and cheese share a quality that made them staples of French food; they travel. Milk sours, fruit and meat spoil, but good bread can last for days, and a cheese, kept cool and well aired, not only survives for months but, sealed inside its rind, improves with age. A rich Camembert is soft to the lightly pressed thumb. The edibility of *vacherin* is judged by the smoothness of its rind. It's only when the golden skin wrinkles into dips and hollows that one can push it aside and spoon out the pungent, runny interior. Cantal, a hard cow's-milk cheese from the Auvergne, is regarded not as a single cheese but three: *jeune* (aged between one and two months), *entre-deux* or *doré* (two to six months), and *vieux* (more than six months.)

Any good Paris *fromager* is usually happy to explain these qualities. A visit to the most prestigious of them, such as Barthélémy (51 rue de Grenelle, in the seventh), which supplies cheese to the presidential palace, can be educational but expensive. Easier for the newcomer to get some sense of regional differences by browsing the street markets.

On Saturday and Sunday mornings, Auvergnat gentlemen may be seen selling charcuterie and cheese on rue de Seine. Often they wear the shepherd's traditional black smock and wide black felt hat. Their stall is heaped with the product of that remote and mountainous province: wind-dried hams, hard salami-like *saucisson* made from *sanglier* (wild boar), and sometimes including *noisettes* (hazelnuts) or *myrtilles* (blueberries).

Their cheeses—mellow Cantal, blue-veined Fourme d'Ambert, and gray-rind Saint-Nectaire— aren't sold in neat shrink-wrapped wedges but from huge wheels. If you appear sufficiently interested, one of the men may take a huge flat knife, slice a sliver, and offer it off the blade to taste.

Are they *really* from the Auvergne? Might they actually work for the butcher just behind their stall, or even for the nearby supermarket? These are not questions it would be polite to ask. As with so many things in France, it is more pleasurable to surrender to the moment, and the fantasy.

RICH MAN, POOR MAN,
BEGGAR MAN . . .

And he took what they gave him, for sore was his need.
(Then he spoke, for he lacked not wit)
'Why give ye me lodging? Why give ye me bread?
Alas, how must I pay for it?'

ALLEGEDLY FROM "THE DOWNFALL OF LORD
AIGHN," AN OLD IRISH BALLAD, BUT INCLUDED
IN CHRISTOPHER ISHERWOOD'S TRANSLATIONS
OF BERTOLT BRECHT'S VERSE FOR *DIE DREI-
GROSCHENOPER (THE THREEPENNY OPERA)* AND
ARGUABLY COMPOSED BY HIM

VISITORS TO PARIS, AFTER HEARING ABOUT THE WHOLE-
sale demolition of entire districts by Baron Haussmann,
sometimes ask, "What become of the people who lived
there?"

Some returned to the districts where their families had

farmed. Paris, like Los Angeles, has always been mostly inhabited by people from somewhere else. Many settled in Montmartre, not then part of greater Paris. Its mills, workshops, barns, and shacks absorbed them like a sponge. As the population of Saint-Germain dropped by half, that of Montmartre doubled. Renoir and his friends painted and partied in an old flour mill; Picasso and Braque developed Cubism in an ancient factory that creaked and leaked so much in bad weather that they named it the Bateau Lavoir, or Laundry Boat, after the hulks on the Seine where washerwomen carried on their trade.

Those who found Montmartre too seedy moved outside the old walls into what became known as *le banlieue*—the suburbs. Others relocated farther out in such satellite towns as Saint-Denis, soon to become part of a "Red Belt" around the city, a community of Communist voters who influenced twentieth-century Parisian politics.

The area between the city and *le banlieue* became known, over the years, as *le zone*. As Saint-Germain grew more prosperous, a few *zonards*, as they were unflatteringly known, have drifted back to the streets from which Haussmann evicted their grandparents. In a left-handed way of reclaiming their birthright, some work as pickpockets, street hustlers, and *mendiants* (beggars).

Monitored by shopkeepers who don't hesitate to

summon the *gendarmerie*, Saint-Germain's beggars are, of necessity, a serene group. Installed at the sunnier corners on boulevard Saint-Germain, often on a blanket and accompanied by a dozy mutt, they ply their trade as politely and professionally as any *boulanger* or *charcutier*.

Can begging be called a trade? Why not? The beggar offers a service: an opportunity, simply by dropping a few coins in a cup, to feel magnanimous and compassionate. Just as, passing a florist, we may pause and ask ourselves, "Should I buy some flowers?," we should, on approaching a panhandler, ask ourselves, "Do I need a beggar today?"

Historically, the beggars of Paris have as much right to the streets as any other resident. For a thousand years, they have been part of Parisian society. In *Notre-Dame de Paris*, Victor Hugo draws a vivid picture of their seventeenth-century haunt, the Cour des Miracles—so called because, away from the public gaze, the apparent amputee miraculously regained his missing limb and the fake blind man his sight.

Beggars also led certain orders of monks to renounce worldly goods, relying on charity. But how typical of the French that some inventive chocolatier should have been inspired by the brown, beige, and white of their homespun habits to create a confection. By embedding a few brown raisins, some slivers of beige dried fruit, and a couple of

Classic Paris beggar on 1890s sheet music.

peeled white almonds in a disc of chocolate, he created the *mendiant*, a popular nibble at Christmas and New Year's.

Recently, a new community of the needy has appeared on the streets of Saint-Germain. Mostly women, they wear the clothing of Eastern Europe: long skirt, shapeless top, scarf tied babushka-style around the head. They show no hand-lettered sign, hold no baby, display no bedraggled dog. Their eyes are sufficient, holding all the sorrow of the modern world. Abstract questions like "Do I need a beggar today?" wilt in the face of their misery. Too often, one looks away, aware that there is a limit to compassion.

❋ ·20· ❋

THE RUMBLE IN THE TUNNEL

Opposing me are the middle-class, the military and the diplomats, while the only people on my side are those who ride the Metro.
CHARLES DE GAULLE

THE METRO HAS MORE THAN THREE HUNDRED STATIONS. Many have been beautified, turning them into tourist attractions, but none so elaborately as Louvre-Rivoli, the stop nearest the great art museum. Almost a gallery in its own right, it's decorated with copies of statues and reliefs ranging from ancient Assyrian tiling to sculptures by Auguste Rodin.

Traditionally, inner-city stations are off-limits to graffiti artists, known as taggers, but one night in April 1991, the temptation proved too great. Hiding in unused tunnels until trains stopped at one a.m., a team calling itself VEP, led by a man with the nickname Oeno, helped by others signing themselves Stem and Gary, lavishly defaced it. Their spray-painted signatures and abstract squiggles were, they announced, "a veritable declaration of war" against RATP, the authority that controls Paris's railways.

The uproar was predictable. Hellfire was called down on the vandals who had attacked these masterpieces, albeit facsimiles, with their *bombes de peinture*. But the indignation didn't take root. Instead, editorials and op-ed pieces in the more thoughtful newspapers suggested that Oeno and his team were simply redressing an imbalance. Hadn't the Impressionists displayed a similar impatience when they boycotted the established salons and held their own Salon des Refusés? Others cited the revolt of the Postimpressionists. When their paintings were exiled to a side gallery where a Donatello statue appeared to shrink from the canvases as from carnivores, didn't they proudly adopt the collective title Les Fauves (The Wild Beasts)?

The discussion went on all week. Writers and critics who hadn't set foot in the Metro since grade school now strolled its platforms, less commuters than connoisseurs. In certain salons of the sixteenth *arrondissement*, where no reference to any painter more recent than Poussin had been permitted for decades, dinner guests compared graffiti artist Jef Aérosol to Jean-Michel Basquiat, and argued the rival abilities of Speedy Graphito and Blek le Rat.

Then, as at a signal, the fun was over. Cleaners went through the Louvre-Rivoli stop, scouring the walls and sculptures. Journalists turned again to the sexual indiscretions of the current president. But an important point had been made. In December 1991, the new minister of culture, Jack Lang, invited the taggers who had attacked the Metro to demonstrate their work as part of an art fair in La Defense, the ultramodern business district on the outskirts of Paris. Graffiti had joined the establishment.

Graffiti at Louvre-Rivoli metro stop, 1991.

THE METRO STATIONS AT ODÉON AND CLUNY–LA SORBONNE

After 1991, RATP accelerated its program to relieve the tedium of the office workers' repetitive *Metro, boulot, dodo* (Metro, job, sleep) by making Metro platforms more interesting. Life-size copies of Rodin's *The Thinker* and his statue of novelist Honoré de Balzac appeared on the platform of Varenne, the station that serves the Rodin museum. At Arts et Métiers, the stop nearest to the city's museum of technology, a platform was sheathed in copper-colored metal and fitted with portholes to evoke Jules Verne's *Twenty Thousand Leagues Under the Sea.*

In Saint-Germain, progress has been slower. The platform hall of the Cluny–La Sorbonne station, built exceptionally wide to accommodate a third set of rails, was decorated with two huge mosaic birds designed by stained-glass artist Jean Bazaine. They sweep across the ceiling, scattering facsimile signatures of fifty distinguished Sorbonne graduates— Racine, Sartre, Abelard, Marie Curie, but also, a little puzzlingly, Maximilien de Robespierre, architect of the Terror.

The Odéon station also has revolutionary associations. Excavated directly under the former home of Georges-Jacques Danton, the site of which is marked by a large statue, the Metro platform enshrines a bust of the revolutionary hero who was executed by Robespierre in 1794. It may seem unfeeling to display just the head of someone decapitated on the guillotine, but Danton wouldn't have minded. Mounting the scaffold, he told the assistant executioner, "Don't forget to show my head to the people. It's well worth seeing."

21

EATING WITH ANAÏS

It was like feasting with panthers. The danger was half the excitement.

OSCAR WILDE, "DE PROFUNDIS"

O<small>N</small> J<small>ANUARY</small> 21, 1793, <small>AS HE WAITED ON THE</small> P<small>LACE DE</small> la Révolution for his turn under the guillotine's blade, Louis XVI asked one of his guards, "Is there any news of Monsieur La Pérouse?"

An odd query for a doomed man, but Louis took a special interest in the fate of Jean-François de Galaup, Comte de La Pérouse, who had set sail in 1785 with two ships, *La Boussole* and *L'Astrolabe*, to continue the epic mapping of the Pacific begun by James Cook but cut short when Hawaiians killed him in 1779.

More enthusiastic about exploration than politics, Louis took personal charge of plans for the voyage. Disturbed when news of its progress dwindled, then died, he would go to the guillotine unaware that La Pérouse and his men were five years dead, both ships wrecked on Vanikoro in the Solomon Islands.

En route to this fate, La Pérouse visited Australia, arriving only a few days after a Royal Navy flotilla planted the British flag and claimed it for George III. Philosophically, the French invited their British opposite numbers to dinner—undoubtedly the best meal they had eaten in a year—and sailed off into oblivion.

In an ambiguous return for his courtesy, Australia attached the name of La Perouse to a dreary stretch of rocky foreshore along Botany Bay, south of Sydney. Like many inner-city kids, I came to know it well since, on Sundays, descendants of the aboriginal people who once had lived there, harvesting local oysters and clams, returned to sell craftwork decorated with the shells of those same mollusks.

Back in the 1950s, when the church in Australia strangled all Sunday entertainment, our parents sometimes drove us out to La Perouse for a picnic. Uninterested in the shell carvings, we kids preferred the demonstrations of boomerang throwing and, even more, of snake handling, the specialty of one family, the members of which arrived with burlap bags wriggling with reptiles. Emptying dozens of them onto the grass, they let the snakes slither around their bodies and, occasionally, bite them as we snapped pictures with our Brownie cameras. Not the tribute Monsieur le Comte de La Pérouse might have hoped from the country he helped literally to put on the map, but we can't all choose our memorials.

Mention the name "La Pérouse" in today's Paris and only one place comes to mind: the stately eighteenth-century mansion overlooking the Seine on the Quai des Grands Augustins that, for more than a century, has housed one of the city's most famous restaurants. Or perhaps the mot juste is "notorious" since the meals at Lapérouse have always been liberally seasoned with vice.

For this, blame a Monsieur Lefèvre, who bought the building after the Revolution and ran it as a wine shop. Recognizing that some clients preferred to share a bottle with an attractive companion but not to be seen doing so, he turned the first-floor rooms of his servants into *salons privés* where they could drink and dine behind closed doors.

According to legend, a tunnel ran from the cellars through the crypts of an old convent next door for those who wished to arrive and leave incognito. Some claimed it reached as far as the Senate, in the old palace of Marie de Médicis on the Jardin du Luxembourg—useful for the many politicians who enjoyed the facilities, among them President François Mitterrand.

When a change in the law recognized adultery only if it took place in a private home, occupancy rates at Lapérouse soared. By 1850, the restaurant had become, as one official history put it, "the rendezvous of all Paris—literary, political and romantic." In 1878, a new owner, Jules Lapérouse, saw a way of enhancing its prestige even more. He renamed the restaurant Lapérouse and transformed it into a memorial to the great explorer. He christened the larger dining rooms Boussole and Astrolabe, after La Pérouse's ships, and decorated the walls with South Seas motifs. When clients assumed some family connection between Monsieur Lapérouse and the count, the restaurateur modestly bowed his head and kept quiet.

The new Lapérouse won a reputation for its food, particularly when the great Escoffier—"king of chefs, and chef to kings"—ran its kitchens, but those *salons privés* remained its most popular attraction. Behind their closed doors, on banquettes upholstered in red velvet, generations of courtesans exercised their skills and young women surrendered their virginity.

The restaurant's reputation survived into the twentieth century. Food critic Julian Street, whose *Where Paris Dines* was indispensible to any gourmet visiting Paris in the 1920s, lavished praise on its menus and cellar, but had almost as much to say about its raffish reputation.

Almost every earnest and discerning eater who has known Paris in the last seventy-five years has at one time or another lunched or dined there. Tradition marks it as a favorite eating place of Thackeray and of Robert Louis Stevenson, and when, a few months after the death of King Ferdinand of Romania, the Prime Minister Bratiano also died and the Crown Prince Carol was reported on his way to Romania where a coup d'etat in his favour was expected, the prince was in fact ensconced in a private dining room at Lapérouse.

Closer to our time, King Edward VIII dined there with his future wife, Wallis Simpson. Orson Welles was a client, and it was here that singer and actor Serge Gainsbourg met Jane Birkin, the leggy young English actress who became his mistress and muse. More recently, Olivier Rousteing, creative director of the fashion house of Pierre Balmain, celebrated the launch of his latest show with a dinner for fifty "besties," including Kim Kardashian, her husband Kanye West, actor Jared Leto, numerous models, and the somewhat curdled cream of Eurotrash society.

I had dined there too, most notably at a dinner in honor of Kitty Carlisle Hart, TV personality and widow of *My*

Fair Lady producer Moss Hart, but never in a *salon privé*. For that experience, I needed someone who shared my relish for the forbidden, the clandestine, the erotic. I had almost given up hope of finding such a person, until I met . . . well, call her Anaïs.

Anaïs has the legs of Tina Turner, the body of Josephine Baker, and the mind of her namesake Anaïs Nin, lover of Henry Miller and author of such erotic classics as *Delta of Venus*. A writer herself, she has no permanent home but lives where her inclinations carry her—sometimes Manhattan, sometimes France.

Though we had only met three of four times, we had become close. About our meetings, there was always a quality of conspiracy. I already knew that her imagination was inexhaustible and her sensual appetite rivaled only by her curiosity. Who better to share this adventure?

And yet a certain *pudeur* made me hesitate. Not to mention . . . well, a little trepidation. Thus might a driver accustomed to Volkswagens contemplate turning the key of a Ferrari.

"How would you feel," I said over a bottle of Pouilly Fumé (her favorite), "about having supper with me in a *salon privé* at Lapérouse."

"A *salon privé*," she said thoughtfully. "How *privé* is that, exactly?"

"Very." I read her a description of Lapérouse from *Where Paris Dines*.

> *A veritable honeycomb of small apartments, it has one private dining room with panels attributed to Boucher and another, also worth seeing, which is a secret cubbyhole for two, with a concealed door opening into the curved wall of a tiny stair landing. The door is made to match the wall and there is no knob, but must be opened with a key carried by a discreet maître d'hotel, and the most jealous of jealous husbands might search the restaurant from top to bottom without discovering the room's existence.*

"Do you suppose there really is such a room?" she asked.

"I can find out."

"Well, if it does . . ." Her dark eyes glinted. Of what they conveyed, the French, as usual had the perfect word. "*Diablerie*." Devilishness.

The *salon privé* with the curved wall does exist, I discovered. It is known as the Salon La Belle Otéro.

Agustina Otéro Iglesias, dancer, actress, and courtesan, known as La Belle (The Beautiful) Otéro, was a legend of the Belle Epoque. Her lovers included Prince Albert I of Monaco, Britain's King Edward VII, the kings of Spain and Serbia, as well as Grand Dukes Peter and Nicholas of Russia, the Duke of Westminster, and writer Gabriele D'Annunzio. Duels were fought over her, and she reportedly drove six men to suicide. Her breasts inspired the cupolas of the Hotel Carlton in Cannes. She died in Nice in 1965, aged ninety-seven. "She was constantly talking about her past," recalled a friend. "It was always the same: feasts, princes, champagne."

On a rainy Friday night two weeks later, I loitered in the ground-floor bar of Lapérouse, spinning out a glass of Bordeaux and watching the rain-swept Quai des Grands Augustins. My only company was the hostess, who diplomatically wandered in and out, for fear that we might be forced to make conversation.

Anaïs was late, but I was used to that. Women have transformed being late into an art that men, if they have any sense, learn to appreciate. The experience of being kept on tenterhooks, of starting at every sound just outside the door, of surrendering to the growing belief that one has been stood up, can be, in itself, the cause of pleasurable excitement.

If one is to wait, few places are more appropriate than the lounge of Lapérouse. Waiting has drenched its red velvet armchairs and banquettes in ennui. During the Belle Epoque, beautiful women crowded the room, most of them *poules de luxe* hoping to snare a free-spending patron. Known as the *plats du jour*—the daily specials—they lingered over a Chartreuse and kept their eye on the staircase. Should a gentleman desire company, the maître d' would come to the door, look around for the kind of woman whom he knew, from experience, to be his client's type, and, catching her eye, touch the mole on his cheek—a signal for her to follow him upstairs.

As I thought about those times, the taped background music switched from Charles Aznavour to Marvin Gaye's "I Heard It Through the Grapevine." Assuming I'd been stood up and was brooding over rejection, the hostess said, "If you wish, I can change . . ."

"No, no . . ."

And as if the music had been her cue, Anaïs swept in, raindrops glittering in her hair, long legs flashing under an abbreviated miniskirt. The song, no longer the yearning appeal of a discarded lover, sounded like an anthem. Noël Coward was right. *Extraordinary how potent cheap music is.*

SALON LA BELLE OTÉRO, LAPÉROUSE, QUAI DES GRANDS AUGUSTINS

Ascending a narrow staircase on the heels of the maître d', I tried and failed to unravel the path that led us to our *salon privé*. We never glimpsed any other clients, nor the restaurant proper where dozens of diners were lingering over their coffee and wondering if they should have a second Courvoisier.

Instead, at the head of the stairs, we found ourselves at the end of a long corridor lined with closed doors.

"*Voilà, 'sieur, mam'zelle,*" said our guide, opening the first door. "*Votre salon.*"

A circular table filled most of the space, flanked by soft-cushioned banquettes. A large mirror framed in gilt hung between the shuttered, curtained window and the wall nearest the door, where it bulged inward to accommodate the curve of the staircase outside: *A secret cubbyhole for two, with a concealed door opening into the curved wall of a tiny stair landing...*

We each subsided onto a banquette. Above

Anaïs's head, the mirror, diplomatically angled, bore a web of ancient scratches—made, traditionally, by women who, offered a diamond for their compliance in some erotic act, first tested it on the glass.

At the height of Olivier Rousteing's party, he and a few of his best "besties" had fled to this exact room. "The group tumbled, puppy-like, onto a velvet sofa," wrote a reporter. "'Take a picture! Take a picture!' Rousteing cried. Laughing and pouting and sucking in their cheeks, they shot selfies and group portraits on their smartphones, then reluctantly went back down to the party, but not before posting shots to their Instagram feeds."

For the next three hours, we ate very little and drank rather too much but the real intoxication was in talk—the only currency traded in Saint-Germain. Confidences were exchanged, memories evoked, sensations explored with the same freedom as sins are whispered in the secrecy of the confessional. In a way never quite achievable even in our bedrooms, we were alone, isolated in a zone where the only rules were those we made ourselves.

From time to time, the press on a button summoned a waiter to clear the plates and bring more wine, but otherwise the staff respected our purchased privacy. Such luxury—to live only in the moment, elevated above the concerns of the everyday; to reach a state where every pleasure seemed achievable; to be, within the limits of the imagination, one's true and total self—who could ask for more? James Joyce called Paris "a lamp for lovers, hung in the wood of the world," and we were, for that moment, bathed in its light and warmth.

22

THE GONE WORLD

There was nowhere to go but everywhere.
JACK KEROUAC, *ON THE ROAD*

"I WONDER," SAID SYLVIA BEACH WHITMAN, "IF YOU could do me a favor."

Even had she not been one of Paris's most attractive and charming women, Sylvia's importance as proprietor of the modern Shakespeare and Company bookshop would have demanded respect.

"Of course," I said. "Name it."

"Jimmy Page is in Paris with his girlfriend," she said, "and he asked for someone to take him on a literary walk. Could you show him around the Luxembourg Gardens?"

"You mean Led Zeppelin's Jimmy Page?" I said. "The Jimmy Page of 'Stairway to Heaven'?"

"Yes. Why. Is that a problem?"

"No," I said. "No, not at all. When do you want to do this?"

"Sunday, if that isn't too soon."

"Let me look at my agenda," I said. I put down the phone and stared at the wall for ten seconds. Then I picked it up again and said, "Yes, I'm free. Where should we meet?"

"Well, could we come by your apartment? Because he also wants to visit the site of the Beat Hotel . . ."

William Burroughs holds court at the Beat Hotel. 1959. (Loomis. Dean/Life)

"THE BEAT HOTEL," CHEZ RACHOU,
NO. 9 RUE GÎT-LE-COEUR

When my girlfriend and I spent our first Paris weekend in that Latin Quarter hotel in 1969, we never
suspected, as we searched for a soft spot in the
mattress while at the same time putting a pillow
over our heads to block the chatter from the cafés
downstairs, that, by Paris standards, we were enjoying moderate luxury.

Hotels were graded on a scale of one to thirteen, on which ours rated about midway. Who knew
that, almost within sight of our room, there existed
an establishment that barely made the lowest cate-
gory? And, even more improbably, attracted some
significant literary figures of the postwar era?

It had no name. Most pedestrians who wandered down the lane from rue Saint-André des
Arts to the quay of the Seine saw only an ill-lit *boîte*
where a handful of drunks and whores loitered away
their evenings.

To rent a room, you applied to the proprietor,
Madame Rachou, behind the bar. Those she admitted found bare board floors that sloped and

creaked, beds with lumpy mattresses, and sheets that, technically, were changed once a month but more like twice a year. Sanitation was represented by a squat toilet on each landing. Bathing was by appointment; a guest had to book the single bathtub a week ahead, but most didn't bother. So weak was the electrical current that, should anyone connect an unauthorized hot plate or radiator, every light bulb in the building dimmed. This would bring an irate Madame Rachou to the door to confiscate the offending appliance.

But the Beat Hotel held the same appeal as the Hôtel Jacob, where the Hemingways stayed in 1921: it was cheap. After veterans studying under the GI Bill discovered its seedy charm and low rates, it became a mecca for those young writers who, no less than Hemingway, Miller, and Pound, believed that simply breathing the air of Paris would inspire greatness. "They were on an island," wrote 1960s student radical Jean-Jacques Lebel, "isolated in this magic little paradise full of rats and bad smells. But it was paradisial because it gave them the green light to be themselves without having to confront America."

Today the building houses the four-star Relais

Hôtel du Vieux Paris. Acknowledging its former literary glory, the management displays photographs of Burroughs, Ginsberg, and Corso, while a plaque rather perfunctorily acknowledges "B. Gysin, H. Norse, G. Corso, A. Ginsberg, P. Orlovsky and I. Sommerville" as former tenants (Harold Norse was a minor poet and Ian Sommerville a computer engineer who worked with Gysin on his optical experiments) and that "W. Burroughs wrote *The Naked Lunch* (1959) here."

From time to time, a city inexplicably becomes *the* place to be. Movie-mad Los Angeles in the 1940s, "Beat" New York in the 1950s, "Swinging" London in the 1970s, Paris in the *années-folles* of the 1920s and again in the 1950s.

The reasons defy analysis. In the years after World War I, when Dada migrated from Zurich to Paris and metamorphosed into surrealism, the community that coalesced around André Breton did so by a process none of its members understood. "There is absolutely no reason." Jean-Claude Carrière, Luis Buñuel's scenarist, told me, "why Benjamin Péret came from Toulouse to join the group, why Max Ernst comes from Germany, why and how Man Ray comes from the States and Buñuel from Spain, and they get together. It was something they shared already before belonging to the same group."

One thing all these groups had in common was the places where they lived. The Surrealists clustered in Montmartre, Montparnasse, and Saint-Germain, then the city's cheapest residential districts. For the Americans of the post–World War II generation, however, rents in those areas were already prohibitive—with one exception: an alley off the Quai des Grands Augustins called rue Gît-le-Coeur, where a couple named Rachou ran the cheapest of cheap hotels.

Many guests of the Rachous belonged to the loose association of experimenters in literature and lifestyle known as the Beat Generation. Poets predominated. Lawrence Ferlinghetti, founder of San Francisco's City Lights bookshop, Gary Snyder, Gregory Corso, and Richard Brautigan all spent time here. Allen Ginsberg and his companion Peter Orlovsky shared a room, and William Burroughs bunked with Brion Gysin, with whom he developed the "cut-up" method of literary creation, scissoring apart sections of text, then juxtaposing them in new and meaningful ways.

Some scraped a living writing pornography for the Olympia Press of Maurice Girodias. From his office on nearby rue de Nesle, Girodias published unapologetic

"DBs"—shorthand for "dirty books." With the profits, he bought new fiction that combined literary merit with varying degrees of salaciousness: Nabokov's *Lolita*, Burroughs's *The Naked Lunch*, Samuel Beckett's *Watt* and *Molloy*, Corso's *American Express*.

As it had been after World War I, Paris in the 1950s was a place to be young and hungry. The few older established writers who passed through took one disbelieving look at the Beat Hotel and didn't linger. In 1965, Jack Kerouac spent a few alcoholic weeks in France looking for the Breton origins of his Quebecois family. To his disappointment, the town from which the Kerouacs emigrated to Canada no longer existed, its only survival the Giratoire de Kervoac, an intersection on a lonely Breton road.

Satori in Paris, the short novel about the journey that became his last, describes half-remembered nights in seedy bars, missed planes and trains, mislaid hotels, and drunken passes at uninterested women. His fellow literary expatriates made a poor impression: "A half-dozen eager or worried future writers, with their manuscripts, all of whom gave me a positively dirty look when they heard my name as tho they were muttering to themselves '*Kerouac*? I can write ten times better than that beatnik maniac.'"

That Sunday—as Jimmy Page and I strolled the Luxembourg Gardens with Louise, and his current girlfriend, the poet Scarlett Sabet—I mused on the fact that, just as he and I were contemporaries, so were Louise and Scarlett. Yet no one would have thought these pairings incongruous. Where other cities encourage the newcomer to "act your age" and "think of your position," Paris urges the opposite: "you are as young as you feel" and "be whoever you wish to be."

Page was wealthy enough to be any place in the world, in any company, and yet he chose to be here? Why? I didn't ask. Instead, as we strolled through the chill gardens of the Luxembourg beside the gray pond, flanked on every side by leafless trees, the talk was of another earlier expatriate in Paris, devil worshipper and self-styled "Great Beast" Aleister Crowley. Page not only owned every scrap of Crowley's work but also once bought Boleskine House, the mansion on the shores of Loch Ness where Crowley lived and performed his satanic rituals. After restoring it at some expense, however, Page sold it, having lived there for only six weeks.

It was a moment to recall what Scott Fitzgerald wrote in one of his stories: "Let me tell you about the very rich. They are different from you and me. They possess and enjoy early, and it does something to them, makes them soft where we are hard, cynical where we are trustful, in a way that, unless you were born rich, it is very difficult to understand."

Not born rich, Page, soft-spoken, friendly, genuinely interested in Paris and its past, radiated an innocence out of tune with this cynical old city—the innocence of Fitzgerald himself, in fact, a man who never felt at home here. Why did so many of the great and gifted leave while we few remained? Were we more coarse-grained, better able to live with the sense felt by all expatriates of exclusion, of always being strangers, outsiders? What then kept us here when Page and Pound and Fitzgerald and Ginsberg and Kerouac and Burroughs moved on? Was it that glimpse of the Panthéon's dome rising above the bare trees, a door swinging ponderously closed on a quiet courtyard, the Seine's gunmetal sheen in autumn twilight, a Parisienne's conspiratorial smile? Whatever it was, we felt more than amply repaid.

An Ordinary Day, with Kalashnikovs

In "Musée des Beaux Arts," his poem suggested by the painting *Landscape with the Fall of Icarus*, W. H. Auden reflected on the almost casual way Pieter Bruegel showed the rash experimenter's end. In the foreground, a plowman gets on with his day. All you see of Icarus and his melting wings is a pair of legs disappearing into the sunny waters.

To Auden, it embodied a truth about disaster.

> *About suffering they were never wrong,*
> *The Old Masters; how well they understood*
> *Its human position; how it takes place*
> *While someone else is eating or opening a window*
>   *or just walking dully along.*

After terrorists attacked Paris on Friday the thirteenth of November, 2015, killing one hundred and thirty people, friends all over the world enquired anxiously after our safety and asked in what way we had been affected.

The question was surprisingly difficult to answer. If I were truthful, I'd say that, until we learned later that night of the atrocities, our day was mainly about cats and a new DVD player.

In midafternoon, the DVD player took precedence. The old one having failed, Louise and I took a crowded bus to Montparnasse and, after plunging through waves of people at least as tumultuous as those that engulfed Icarus, emerged with a new and surprisingly cheap Sony. Whereupon Louise left me to carry it home while she went off "on a stroll."

Arriving on rue de l'Odéon brought the evening's first note of disaster. Just as I opened our door, a neighbor knocked to tell me that, while the owner was in Japan, burglars had broken into the fourth-floor apartment once occupied by Sylvia Beach, proprietor of the original Shakespeare and Company bookshop and publisher of *Ulysses*.

Compared with what came later, the event would appear trivial, but at the time it confronted us with a multitude of difficulties, foremost among them capturing our neighbor's two cats, which, having escaped through the smashed door, were prowling the stairs.

As the sun set—and, as I would later reflect, men on the far side of the city buckled on their explosive vests and checked their Kalashnikovs—we were busy trapping the errant felines, locking them in our own apartment and keeping them separate from our own cat Scotty while at the same time calling our neighbor in Kyoto with the bad news and contacting her housekeeper (who speaks only Romanian) in order to track down our neighbor's son, the polar explorer Sebastian Copeland. You would not think a two-meter-tall person could be hard to find, but Paris, though charmingly open—too open, in hindsight—can, as we would learn that night, harbor all manner of secrets.

By the time we'd eaten a quick dinner, the worst appeared to be over. The tearful calls to and from Japan were completed, the stolen jewelry lamented. As a carpenter boarded up the broken door and replaced the lock, the gendarme from the prefecture suggested the thieves were probably the same Eastern Europeans who had burgled the building last year.

But what about the expensive new security gate and videophone installed after that attack?

He shrugged. "We think they climbed over the wall from the courtyard next door."

Ridiculously in retrospect, I remember feeling insulted by the obviousness of their method, the lack of finesse. Smash, kick, kill. The crude solutions of lesser minds.

Only then, with all apparently dealt with and under control, the cats contented, even the new DVD player installed, did my sister-in-law call.

"Is Louise there?" she asked anxiously. "Are you safe?" And the television began to ooze the horror that would dominate the night.

I sat and watched for hours while Louise rang around to her friends, with whom she'd often attended concerts at the Bataclan. Happily, all were safe.

Disbelief muffled understanding. This couldn't be happening *here*. Journalists assigned to the story appeared to succumb to the same numbness. Posted only a couple of blocks from the Bataclan, the BBC's chief correspondent rambled to the camera on the improbabilities of the attacks, unaware that police had already burst in to find the hundred dead—the horror taking place, just as Auden said, "while someone else is eating or opening a window or just walking dully along."

Maybe it was the thought of Bruegel and Auden and the old masters that made me dig out the DVDs of *Civilisation*, the 1969 BBC documentary series in which art historian Kenneth Clark assessed the intellectual progress of man. I hadn't watched it in decades, but on this night it was as consoling as the Bible to a believer.

Clark, standing alone on the sunny bank of the Seine,

with Notre Dame behind him, began by suggesting that it was "a good moment to look at some of the ways that man has shown himself to be an intelligent, creative, orderly, and compassionate animal." Even more so than half a century ago, this made just as much sense.

I watched for hours as he enumerated barely a fraction of the works of the creative mind—Chartres, Florence, Dutch painting, English music; Wren, Bach, Picasso: each a further proof that civilization cannot be extinguished, least of all by so crude a tool as physical violence. War, plague, bigotry, fanaticism, and genocide might stifle, but they can never destroy. Not the human spirit, and certainly not Paris.

Acknowledgments

I'M PARTICULARLY GRATEFUL TO OUR FRIENDS AND NEIGHbors in Saint Germain for their help in writing this book, in particular Penelope Casadesus, Jim Carroll, Sylvia Beach Whitman and all the staff at the Shakespeare and Company bookshop, and Terrance Gelenter of Paris Through Expatriate Eyes. Also Christopher Jones, Pierre de Coubertin, Ryan Barrett, W. Scott Haine, and Bertram Gordon. Special thanks to Tony Foster, for his tireless work on the map, and, as always, to my editor, Peter Hubbard, as well as Nick Amphlett and all at HarperPerennial—not forgetting my ever-patient agent Jonathan Lloyd at Curtis Brown.

Photo Credits

Unless otherwise noted, photographs are by the author, Louise Baxter, and Robert Doisneau.

INDEX

Note: Italicized page numbers indicate photographs and illustrations.

ABOUT THE AUTHOR

JOHN BAXTER has lived in Paris for more than twenty years. He is the author of six critically acclaimed books about France: *Five Nights in Paris: After Dark in the City of Light*, *The Perfect Meal: In Search of the Lost Tastes of France* (winner of the IACP Cookbook Award for Culinary Travel), *The Most Beautiful Walk in the World: A Pedestrian in Paris*, *Immoveable Feast: A Paris Christmas*, *Paris at the End of the World*, and *We'll Always Have Paris: Sex and Love in the City of Light*. Baxter, who gives literary walking tours through Paris, is also a film critic and biographer whose subjects have included the directors Federico Fellini, Stanley Kubrick, Woody Allen, and, most recently, Josef von Sternberg. Born in Australia, Baxter lives with his wife and daughter in the Saint-Germain-des-Prés neighborhood, in the building Sylvia Beach once called home.

www.johnbaxterparis.com

BOOKS BY JOHN BAXTER

THE PERFECT MEAL
Available in Paperback and E-book

IACP COOKBOOK AWARD WINNER (*Culinary Travel*)

"Full of humor, insight, and mouth-watering details, *The Perfect Meal* is a delightful tour of 'traditional' French culture and cuisine." —*Travel + Leisure*

THE MOST BEAUTIFUL WALK IN THE WORLD
A Pedestrian in Paris

Available in Paperback and E-book

NATIONAL BESTSELLER

Baxter reveals the most beautiful walks through Paris, including the favorite routes of artists and writers who have called the city home.

IMMOVEABLE FEAST
A Paris Christmas

Available in Paperback and E-book

The charming, funny, and improbable tale of how a man who was raised on white bread—and didn't speak a word of French—ended up preparing the annual Christmas dinner for a venerable Parisian family.

WE'LL ALWAYS HAVE PARIS
Sex and Love in the City of Light

Available in Paperback and E-book

"A charming insider's guide to literary and artistic Paris. . . . Excellent." —*Daily Mail* (London)

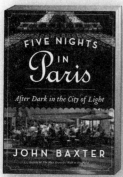

FIVE NIGHTS IN PARIS
After Dark in the City of Light
Available in Paperback and E-book

John Baxter enchanted readers with his literary tour of Paris in *The Most Beautiful Walk in the World*. Now, this expat who has lived in the City of Light for more than twenty years introduces you to the city's streets after dark, revealing hidden treasures and unexpected delights as he takes you through five of the city's greatest neighborhoods.

PARIS AT THE END OF THE WORLD
The City of Light During the Great War, 1914-1918
Available in Paperback and E-book

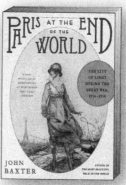

John Baxter brings to life one of the most dramatic and fascinating periods in Paris's history. As World War I ravaged France, the City of Light blazed more brightly than ever. Despite the terrifying sounds that could be heard from the capital, Parisians lived with urgency and without inhibition. The rich hosted wild parties, artists such as Picasso reached new heights, and the war brought a wave of foreigners, including Ernest Hemingway, to Paris for the first time. In this brilliant book, Baxter shows how the Great War forged the spirit of the city we love today.

CARNAL KNOWLEDGE
Baxter's Concise Encyclopedia of Modern Sex
Available in Paperback and E-book

A veritable smorgasbord of sin, John Baxter's *Carnal Knowledge* is a delightfully unabashed education in sex and erotic culture. Would you ever consent to a knee-trembler at a love hotel? Would you enjoy a hot lunch while watching kinbaku? Would you consider wearing a French tickler, a merkin, a strap-on, or pasties . . . or would you rather just go commando at the Mine Shaft? From *Deep Throat* to *Debbie Does Dallas*, from the mile-high club to the Emperor's Club, John Baxter explains it all to you in this decadently definitive work.